Managing Your Own Learning at University

To Angela and Kevin, with all my love.

Managing Your Own Learning at University

A PRACTICAL GUIDE
THIRD EDITION

AIDAN MORAN

UNIVERSITY COLLEGE DUBLIN PRESS
PREAS CHOLÁISTE OLLSCOILE BHAILE ÁTHA CLIATH
2018

First published in 1997 by
University College Dublin Press
Third Edition 2018

© Aidan Moran, 1997, 2000, 2018
Illustrations © Shane Sutton, 1997

ISBN 978-1-910820-26-1

University College Dublin Press
UCD Humanities Institute, Belfield,
Dublin 4, Ireland
www.ucdpress.ie

10 9 8 7 6 5 4 3 2

CIP data available from the British Library

The right of Aidan Moran to be identified as
the author of this work has been asserted by him

Typeset in Plantin and Gill Sans by Ryan Shiels
Text design by Ryan Shiels
Printed in England on acid-free paper by
CPI Antony Rowe, Chippenham, Wiltshire

CONTENTS

Preface and Acknowledgements vii

1 Going to University 1
The Challenge of Managing Your Own Learning

2 Getting Down to Study 15
Motivating Yourself and Developing a Habit of Learning

3 Managing Your Study Time Effectively 33
How Much? How Often? For How Long?

4 Learning from Lectures and Virtual Learning 47
Environments
Practical Tips

5 Tackling Textbooks 73
Improving Your Reading and Summarising Skills

6 How to Focus Effectively 91
Improving Your Concentration Skills

7 Learning to Think Critically 105
Being Sceptical of What You Hear and Read

8 Remembering and Understanding 125
Principles and Practical Tips

9 Managing Research Assignments 149
Projects, Talks and Poster Presentations

10 Doing Your Best in Exams 177
Overcoming the Challenges of Assessment

Glossary 200
References 204
Index 213

PREFACE AND ACKNOWLEDGEMENTS

Going to university is a daunting experience for many students. Why? Because you're confronted with a number of academic challenges for which you have received little or no formal training either in school or at work. For example, you have to learn how to take useful notes in lectures, how to study effectively, how to think critically about what you hear and read, and how to write and deliver research-based assignments. But, above all, you have to *manage your own learning*, a task that involves systematically planning, conducting and evaluating your academic work in university – that is, thinking for yourself. The purpose of this book is to help you to overcome this challenge by giving you practical tips on the science of effective learning.

I've organised this book so that each chapter addresses a different mental challenge or learning skill in university. To begin with, in Chapter 1, I explore the task of 'managing your own learning' which involves becoming an active, independent and self-motivated student. This chapter also introduces a key theme of the book – the idea that effective study requires you to read with a purpose or to look for specific answers to specific questions. Then, in successive chapters, I address such skills as motivating yourself to study (Chapter 2); organising your study time (Chapter 3); learning from lectures and 'virtual learning environments' or VLEs (Chapter 4); improving your reading and summarising skills (Chapter 5); improving your concentration skills (Chapter 6); learning to think critically about what you hear and read (Chapter 7); improving your ability to remember and understand new information (Chapter 8); managing research assignments, talks and poster presentations (Chapter 9); and doing your best in examinations (Chapter 10).

What's new in the third edition of this book? Firstly, I've extensively rewritten the text and included many new research references to ensure that the content and coverage are as accurate and up-to-date as possible. Secondly, I've included lots of new topics. For example,

I explore key transition tips for adapting to university life (Chapter 1); the 'marshmallow challenge' (Chapter 2); the importance of digital tools as part of your university learning experience (Chapter 4); how to overcome digital distractions when studying (Chapter 6); dispelling some pervasive neuromyths (Chapter 7); practical tips on giving talks and making poster presentations (Chapter 9); and how to manage multiple choice exams (MCQs; see Chapter 10). Thirdly, I've compiled a glossary for the book to explain important technical terms. Finally, the artwork and layout have been redesigned to make the book as attractive and as easy to use as possible.

This book would not have been possible without the generous help and wisdom of many colleagues and friends. Therefore, I wish to acknowledge with sincere gratitude the assistance that I received from the following people in recent times: Dr Helen O'Shea, who not only contributed material for Chapters 4 and 9 but whose friendship, scholarly insights and support knew no bounds; Ruth Hallinan (Acting Executive Editor, UCD Press), Noelle Moran (Executive Editor, UCD Press) and Conor Graham (Editorial Assistant, UCD Press), whose gentle editorial suggestions, stylistic advice and constant encouragement enhanced the manuscript greatly; and Colin Burke (Chief Technical Officer, UCD School of Psychology) for his enthusiasm, friendship and technical wizardry. In addition, I wish to thank the following colleagues and friends from the School of Psychology, UCD, for offering advice and suggestions for this book: Full Professor Alan Carr, Assistant Professor Amanda Fitzgerald, Associate Professor Suzanne Guerin, Assistant Professor Ciara Greene and Assistant Professor Brendan Rooney. I also wish to acknowledge with deep gratitude the research assistance award that I received from UCD College of Social Sciences and Law.

Finally, I wish to thank my wife, Angela, my son, Kevin, and my siblings, Ciarán, Dermot and Patricia, for their wonderful love, support, patience and kindness at all times.

Aidan Moran
Dublin, August 2018

EDUCATION IS ONE OF THE FEW THINGS THAT A PERSON IS WILLING TO PAY FOR AND NOT GET.

W. L. Bryan

Chapter 1

Going to University

The Challenge of Managing Your Own Learning

INTRODUCTION

Going to university is an exciting yet intimidating experience for many students. The excitement comes from the adventure of exploring interesting subjects in a new and stimulating educational environment as well as from the fun of making new friends and acquiring different skills and interests. Unfortunately, this expansion of your intellectual and social horizons does not come without a price. In this regard, I'm not referring to the financial cost of your books, computer, accommodation and living and travel expenses. Instead, what I have in mind is the daunting *psychological* challenge that you face when studying any subject in university. You will have to accept personal responsibility for achieving a successful academic education, a task for which you have received little or no special training in school. This task requires you to manage your own learning: to become active, independent, self-motivated and successful in planning, conducting and evaluating your academic work. Accepting this challenge means that you will have to become a driver rather than a passenger in your journey through university. Therefore, the purpose of this book is to give you some 'driving lessons' in learning. The first lesson concerns the type of learning – called active learning – that is required of you in university.

This chapter is organised as follows:

••

➤ I'll explain the nature and characteristics of active learning.

➤ I'll help you to evaluate your current study habits so that you can determine whether they reveal an accidental or a deliberate approach to learning.

➤ I'll introduce a central theme of this book which is the idea that effective study requires reading with a purpose: namely, to obtain specific answers to specific questions.

➤ I'll provide a brief overview of the academic challenges that you can expect to face in university. These challenges include such tasks as:

• Motivating yourself to get down to studying (Chapter 2)
• Managing your study time effectively (Chapter 3)
• Listening and taking lecture notes at the same time and how digital learning plays a part in university (Chapter 4)
• Improving your reading and summarising skills (Chapter 5)
• Improving your concentration skills (Chapter 6)
• Learning to think critically about your subject (Chapter 7)
• Understanding and remembering what you learn (Chapter 8)
• Managing research assignments, talks and poster presentations (Chapter 9)
• Doing your best in essay-style and multiple-choice examinations (Chapter 10).

••

At first glance, many of the academic skills covered in this book may seem familiar to you. After all, you would not be attending university now if you had not shown some prior competence in learning. But it is a big mistake to assume that the learning habits that you have developed in school will automatically guarantee you academic success in university. For a start, do you think that you will you be able to motivate yourself to study in the absence of such familiar school 'props' as prescribed textbooks, a largely standardised syllabus and daily inspection of your homework? Similarly, if you're entering university from the workplace, you won't have a manager organising deadlines for your work on a weekly or monthly basis.

Next, are you prepared for the fact that the amount of time that you will spend in lectures is relatively low compared to that which you are expected to spend in private study? Clearly, this situation is quite different from what you experienced in school or how team projects in workplaces are organised. Furthermore, how will you know when to give your own opinions of topics or theories rather than a summary of what is contained in your textbooks? Not surprisingly, the success of your education in university will depend on the way in which you answer these questions. That is why universities are paradoxical – they bring out the *best* and *worst* qualities in students simultaneously.

But it all makes sense when you realise that universities make demands of you at two different levels – the **cognitive** and the **metacognitive**.

If you're not prepared to take responsibility for your own learning at each of these two levels, university will be a frustrating and unhappy experience for you. However, if you relish the challenge of developing new knowledge and skills, then you will flourish in university.

The choice is yours. So, let's take some driving lessons in learning.

LEARNING: ACTIVE (DELIBERATE) AND INCIDENTAL (UNPLANNED)

The term '**learning**' refers to a relatively permanent change in our knowledge and/or our behaviour as a result of experience. For example, consider how we learn to drive a car. In this case, the experience is a programme of driving lessons, the change in knowledge involves an increased understanding of what driving involves, and the change in behaviour refers to the skills of actually starting, steering and stopping the car safely.

It would be a mistake to assume that the 'understanding' and 'doing' parts of behaviour can ever be separated completely. They go hand-in-hand. For example, learning to play tennis requires both **conceptual knowledge** and **procedural skills**.

Learning can be **deliberate** or **incidental**. Deliberate learning is usually motivated by a clear and specific purpose whereas incidental learning happens by chance. For example, the clear and specific goal of wanting to drive a car leads to the motivation of taking planned driving lessons. By contrast, incidental learning could occur if you take a wrong turn down a road and thereby discover a shortcut home.

By the way, as a test of your incidental learning ability, did you happen to notice the name of the publisher of this book? No? Well, look for it now! Since you're looking for the name of the publisher because I asked you to, you have begun to engage in deliberate learning.

This distinction between deliberate and incidental learning has profound practical significance. Research shows that the knowledge produced by a *deliberate intention* to answer a question connects strongly with what we already know. This connection produces a richer and more durable long-term memory (see Chapter 8) than that yielded by random browsing (Dunlosky et al., 2013). As we shall see, this finding explains why active engagement through *questioning* before you read a book (i.e. 'What exactly am I trying to find out here?') promotes deeper understanding of the material than does passive reading of it.

Of course, incidental learning such as browsing online can be valuable also. Interestingly, the history of science is replete with serendipitous discoveries. For example, in 1941, George de Mestral allegedly invented the 'Velcro' fastener after he had noticed that burs stuck to his clothing during a walk in the woods. Similarly, Bernard Sadow created wheeled luggage in 1970 when he saw a man pushing machinery on a trolley through an airport. What is intriguing about these 'chance' discoveries is that they tend to occur most frequently to people who are *actively* searching for answers to questions – whether consciously or unconsciously. There is great wisdom in aphorisms like 'Luck happens when preparation meets opportunity' or 'Fortune favours the prepared mind'.

BECOMING AN ACTIVE LEARNER: MAKING THE TRANSITION FROM SCHOOL TO UNIVERSITY

So far, I've highlighted the importance of active learning in generating rich and durable knowledge. But this type of learning has another major benefit: it can actually help you to make a smooth transition from school to university. To achieve this goal, you'll need to take three steps.

- You will have to learn the importance of curiosity (the drive to explore and understand; Leslie, 2014) and of asking lots of questions. As I'll explain throughout this book, effective studying is based on questioning. More precisely, it occurs when you look for specific answers to specific questions.

- You will have to learn a variety of mental skills. These skills include how to motivate yourself, how to organise your time, how to focus effectively, how to understand things better and how to think critically.

- You'll have to be willing to learn from the experience of others, especially relevant experts. For example, here are some experts' 'transition tips' for new university students. See Box 1.1 below.

Box 1.1 Transition tips: What you need to know and do to adapt to university life

---

1 Get involved in university life as quickly as possible because this widens your circle of friends and improves your sense of belonging and wellbeing. This could take the form of joining a sports team or taking part in a society.

2 Attend all of your lectures – even if the slides are available online – because otherwise you'll miss the questions, comments and discussions that challenge your brain. Class attendance is strongly related to academic success.

3 Keep your laptop and phone in your bag during lectures to avoid distractions from social media and browsing online (See Chapter 4).

4 Ask for help from the faculty or learning support services and the Students' Union if you have problems or any concerns about your mental health.

5 Make your time in university as memorable as possible by stretching your mind, having fun and enjoying the adventure.

(Putnam et al., 2016; Rhodes, 2017)

Now that you understand how to become an active learner, you need to evaluate your current study habits.

EVALUATING YOUR STUDY HABITS

In order to improve any skill, you have to first evaluate your own performance. In Box 1.2, I would like you to establish whether your current study habits reflect a 'deliberate' or an 'incidental' approach to learning.

Box 1.2 Are you a deliberate or incidental learner?

Consider your present study habits. To find out if they reflect deliberate or incidental learning, please answer either 'yes' or 'no' to the following questions. Be honest! There is no point in fooling yourself.

QUESTIONS

1   Do you have a clear plan or timetable for your studies each day? (y/n)

2   Do you write down specific questions on a blank sheet of paper before you read a book or article that you wish to study? (y/n)

3   Before you read a chapter, do you flick through it to get a quick overview of what it's about? (y/n)

4   Do you check your progress as you study by asking yourself how the new material relates to what you already know? (y/n)

5   Do you always write summaries of important points as you read a book? (y/n)

6   When you have finished studying, do you take a moment to review what you have learned? (y/n)

If you answered 'yes' to most of the questions in Box 1.2, then your present study habits are probably quite efficient so there is little need to change what you're doing.

However, if you answered 'no' to most of these questions, then your current study habits are probably *incidental* rather than deliberate. This suggests that you're not likely to remember much of what you learn. Therefore, what you need is a practical way of making your learning *more deliberate* and focused than it is at present. The best way to do this is to develop the habit of *asking specific questions* before you read your textbooks or notes.

READING, STUDYING AND QUESTIONING: HOW TO TACKLE A TEXTBOOK

Most people regard 'reading' and 'studying' as equivalent terms. After all, both activities involve making sense of text on a page or screen. Although these terms seem similar, they actually refer to very different processes. **Cognitive psychologists** have discovered that studying is a more complex mental activity than reading. Studying involves considerable mental effort and conscious control because you have to keep a question in mind as you read. In addition, studying requires you to filter what you're reading for its relevance to your question. You're constantly checking if what you're reading answers your question or not. By contrast, once you have learned the skill of reading, it is largely an automatic process that requires very little mental effort or conscious control. In a nutshell, studying is *always* hard work mentally – and has to be for it to be effective – but reading is relatively easy once you know how. The lesson is clear: while you can read without studying (as many people do!), you can't study effectively without reading.

What does the difference between reading and studying have to do with tackling a textbook? Let's imagine what would happen if you tried to read a textbook as if it were a novel. Opening the book, you would sit down and begin to read the pages sequentially. And because you're approaching it as if it were a novel, you would not take any notes. Unfortunately, if you did this, your mind would soon begin to wander. Why? Because textbooks are *not designed* to be read like novels – they are meant to be consulted over time rather than processed at one sitting. Accordingly, textbooks contain features that are not found in novels such as a table of contents, a reference section and a subject and author index. These features enable textbooks to be *interrogated* by people who are looking for specific answers to specific questions.

The best way to tackle a textbook is to look upon it as something that you're *consulting* or looking up in an effort to *find answers* to questions. Imagine your study questions are 'a) What is photosynthesis, and b) how does it work?' In order to answer these questions, you write them on a sheet of paper and then you flick through your biology textbook until you find information that seems relevant. You write the information down on a sheet of paper underneath the two questions. When you're finished, you should repeat the same steps with a *different* biology book and compare the answers that you obtain. As you can see from this example, studying always involves active *questioning*, whereas reading for leisure is usually less focused

Curiosity is a key cognitive skill that separates successful students from less successful peers. In addition, research shows that these two types of students differ in other ways as they read a textbook (Dembo & Seli, 2016). For example, as Box 1.3 indicates, successful students tend to flick back and forth to check that they actually understand what they're reading (a skill called '**comprehension monitoring**') and they also slow down when they come across difficult material. By contrast, unsuccessful students rarely check their understanding as they read.

A powerful practical tip arises from these findings. As you read a textbook, ask yourself questions like: *Is this material new to me or not? What does it remind me of? How does it fit in with what I already know? Overall, what's the main idea I'm learning from this chapter?*

Box 1.3 How successful and unsuccessful students read a textbook

Reading a Textbook	
Successful students *Active approach*	*Unsuccessful students* *Passive approach*
Use questions to guide their reading (e.g. turn chapter and paragraph headings into questions for themselves)	Read without questions
Flick back and forth between the pages looking for answers	Read material in a strict, chronological sequence
Slow down when they encounter difficulty and re-read difficult sections	Read at same pace regardless of difficulty of material
Check their understanding	Rarely check

WHY ASKING QUESTIONS IMPROVES YOUR LEARNING

Asking questions improves your learning for at least three reasons.

1 It prepares your mind and sharpens your concentration by giving you a specific target (the question) at which to aim your 'mental spotlight' (see Chapter 6). The clearer and more specific your question, the easier it will be to concentrate on information that could answer it.

2 Research shows that asking questions before you read something increases your memory and understanding of it. To illustrate, consider the **self-reference effect** (Symons & Johnson, 1997). To experience this effect, see Box 1.4.

3 Asking questions encourages you to *think critically* about what you read because it compels you to distinguish between relevant information that helps to answer your question and irrelevant material that has no bearing on it. For example, if your study question is 'What were the main causes of the French Revolution?', then it makes little sense to become side-tracked by events, no matter how interesting, that happened after this era.

For these three reasons, writing down your study questions before you open a textbook or article helps you to think while you are reading.

Box 1.4 The self-reference effect: Why it's good to ask 'What's in it for me?'

Read the following list of words aloud to a small group of people (Group 1) and ask them to listen carefully while you speak:

Brave; humorous; loyal; cold; arrogant; aggressive; sincere; confident; trustworthy

Then, unexpectedly, about 30 minutes later, ask them to write down as many of these words as they can remember. Write down the words they recall correctly.

Repeat the procedure with a different group of people (Group 2), but, this time, tell them that you want them to think about whether or not each of these adjectives applies accurately to them. As before, write down the words this group can recall when prompted unexpectedly about 30 minutes later. You will find that Group 2 recalls significantly more words than Group 1 because the act of checking whether or not something applies to yourself improves your memory.

In short, asking, 'What's in it for me?' pays off! Why? Relating information to yourself helps to elaborate new material and to 'glue' it to what you already know or believe. A practical implication of this effect is that it's easier to use personally meaningful numbers rather than random ones when setting a security PIN (e.g. your birthday).

Asking questions transforms passive or aimless reading into active or deliberate learning. But apart from being able to question what you read, let's examine what other academic skills you will be expected to master in university.

THE ACADEMIC CHALLENGES OF UNIVERSITY: TEACHING, STUDYING AND ASSESSMENT

There are many differences between the academic demands of school and university. To begin with, you will encounter different teaching methods in university from those that you experienced in school. These include lectures, small tutorial groups and group work that will impose new demands on you. For instance, accurate note-taking at lectures requires you to perform two apparently incompatible skills at the same time – listening and writing. But, as I'll explain in Chapter 4, there are certain strategies that will help you to become proficient in note-taking. For example, writing notes by hand pays off – research shows that students who hand-write their notes at a lecture can recall more information from it than did those who take notes on their computers (Mueller & Openheimer, 2014).

A second new challenge of university is that it requires you to engage in far more independent study than you did in school. For example, you need to consult a variety of different sources for your research assignments instead of relying on just a few prescribed textbooks (see also Chapter 9).

Thirdly, you will encounter different types of exams (e.g. multiple-choice questions, also known as MCQs) and different criteria of evaluation from those which you experienced in school. This discovery may initially prove rather disconcerting. For example, you may be shocked to receive a mark of only 50 per cent for a project or essay for which you usually receive 85 per cent in school. If you've been disappointed by a major discrepancy between expected and actual marks, then it's important to seek advice from your professors about how to improve your work. More generally, here's an exercise to help you to think about some key learning skills that you will need in university (see Box 1.5).

Box 1.5 Some learning skills in university

Below are some learning skills that you will encounter in university. Please indicate for each one whether or not you have received any formal training in it to date.

Learning skill: Have you ever been trained in it?	(y/n)
Motivating myself to study	
Planning and adhering to my study timetables	
Taking notes in lectures	
Taking notes from books or journals	
Thinking critically about what I hear or read	
Learning how to use the library	
Learning how to concentrate	
Remembering and understanding what I learn	
Researching and writing essays, projects or papers	
Using technology for learning	
Presenting material to an audience	

As with Box 1.1, if you gave a majority of 'yes' responses, you are fortunate to be well-prepared for the intellectual demands of university. But, if your answers were mostly 'no', then you need some help with your learning skills. As you will discover, it is precisely those skills for which you received *least* training in school that will exert the greatest influence on your academic success in university. But take heart – help is at hand! In the remainder of this book, I'll explain a self-regulation system that will help you to manage your own learning; that is, to become an active, independent and successful student in university.

SUMMARY

In this chapter, I proposed that one of the biggest academic challenges that you will encounter in university is that of managing your own learning – becoming an active, self-motivated and successful student. Unfortunately, this task is one for which you have received little or no formal training during your school years. Furthermore, it will make demands of you at two different levels – the *cognitive* and the *metacognitive*. In order to make a smooth transition from school to university, you'll need to work on both of these levels at the same time. To achieve this objective, three steps are required.

Be curious

Ask specific questions before you read a paper or book because, if you don't have a question, you're not studying. Psychologically, questioning is the key to active learning: it improves your concentration, memory and understanding.

Learn key mental skills

These skills include how to motivate yourself, how to organise your time, how to focus effectively and how to think critically about what you hear or read.

Take advice from others

Listening to advice, especially from relevant experts, is central to successfully adjusting to university life. Key transition tips include getting involved in university clubs and societies, attending all of your lectures, leaving your phone or laptop in your bag in order to avoid distractions while in lectures and seeking help for any academic or personal problems that may arise.

THE SECRET OF GETTING AHEAD IS GETTING STARTED.

Mark Twain

Chapter 2

Getting Down to Study

Motivating Yourself and Developing a Habit of Learning

INTRODUCTION

Have you ever experienced an irresistible urge to tidy your room, check social media or have another cup of coffee when you're faced with the task of reading a textbook or working on an academic assignment? If so, you've allowed **displacement activities** to prevent you from getting down to academic work. But you are not alone. Overcoming inertia is a constant battle for anyone faced with such ill-defined and time-consuming tasks as studying a textbook or writing an essay or research report. After all, very few people wake up thinking, 'I *really* feel like studying today!' But just because you're rarely in the mood to study doesn't mean that you can't work in a determined and productive manner. In this regard, consider the wisdom of William James in 1890, widely acclaimed as the founder of modern psychology: 'It's easier to act your way into a feeling than to feel your way into action.' In other words, our behaviour often determines our mood – not the other way around. Mindful of this idea, several novelists have been noted as saying 'I write when I'm inspired, and I see to it that I'm inspired at nine o'clock every morning!' Clearly, they discovered that adhering to a strict daily work routine is a powerful antidote to lethargy (O'Toole, 2013). So, what works best in motivating you to get down to study? The purpose of this chapter is to provide some practical answers to this question.

This chapter is organised as follows:

••

➤ I'll help you to understand your motivation in attending university.

➤ I'll explore the nature, types and origins of motivation in your academic life.

➤ I'll explain three ways in which you can increase your motivation to study:

• You can use self-administered rewards as positive reinforcement to strengthen your study habits.

• You can use goal-setting principles to establish specific, challenging and measurable targets for your learning.

• You can re-organise your study environment and improve your pre-study behavioural habits.

••

ASSESSING YOUR MOTIVATION TO STUDY AND WHY 'GRIT' MATTERS

Why did you come to university? In order to explore this question, please try the exercise in Box 2.1.

Box 2.1 Exploring your motivation to attend university

Please read each of the statements below and then indicate your level of agreement with them by using a five-point rating scale where 1 = 'does not apply to me at all' and 5 = 'is very accurate'. To benefit from this exercise, you must be completely honest in your ratings. There are no right or wrong answers.

I came to university because ...	Rating
1 I wanted to improve my education in a specific field.	
2 My parents or family put pressure on me to go to university.	
3 It enables me to develop and mature as a person.	
4 It fills in the time for me until I know what I really want to do.	

5	It provides a great opportunity to learn new things.	
6	I just wanted to get away from home.	
7	I liked the idea of being free for a few years more.	
8	I didn't want to waste my Leaving Certificate points.	
9	A university degree is a sign of achievement for me.	
10	The career I want to pursue requires a university degree.	

Have you answered all of the questions? If so, can you detect any pattern in your responses? Notice that statements 2, 4, 6, 7 and 8 reflect a rather passive orientation with externally-motivated reasons for going to university whereas statements 1, 3, 5, 9 and 10 reflect a more self-motivated and 'internal' approach.

The exercise in Box 2.1 is important because your reasons for attending university provide the motivational foundation on which your studies will be built. As you might expect, motivational factors play a significant role in determining academic success in university. Unfortunately, the selection tests that you sat for entry to university assess your intellectual ability more than your *motivation*. But, as the challenge of managing your own learning demands discipline, focus, perseverance and resilience, it's your **'grit'** rather than your IQ that counts in the end. The term 'grit' is associated with the work of Angela Duckworth, and, for Duckworth (2017), grit involves passion in action or making a commitment to finish what you start, to bounce back from setbacks (resilience), and to exert a sustained effort in practising things that you're not good at in order to achieve success. This raises the question of how motivation, success and practice are related.

MOTIVATION, SUCCESS AND DELIBERATE PRACTICE

Derived from the Latin word *movere* ('to move'), motivation is concerned with all the factors that initiate, direct and sustain our behaviour. Accordingly, a motive is a want or a need that moves us to act in certain ways. For example, in university, you might want to study a topic because you find it fascinating in itself (in-trinsic motivation) or need to cover it because it's on the course and could feature in a forthcoming examination (extrinsic motivation).

Motivation plays a vital role in determining success in any field – especially when it comes to practice. Psychologists distinguish between two types of practice: **generic** (or mindless) and **deliberate** (or mindful). Generic practice is the mindless, effortless repetition of skills that you can already perform quite well. By contrast, deliberate practice involves a purposeful, focused and systematic effort to improve the skills that you can't perform well, or at all, at present (Ericsson, Krampe, & Tesch-Romer, 1993). Extrapolating from the research of Ericsson et al. (1993), Gladwell (2009) claims that it takes at least 10,000 hours of dedicated, deliberate practice to become an expert performer in any field. This is equivalent to about 10 years if you practise for about three hours a day. How can you engage in deliberate practice? See Box 2.2 for some practical tips.

Box 2.2 Practical tips on deliberate practice

1 Here are three practical tips on engaging in deliberate practice (from Ericsson & Pool, 2016): Challenge yourself with activities and skills that are just beyond your comfort zone (the things that you're weak at right now) and be prepared to exert effort in doing so.

2 Set specific goals for yourself and monitor your progress from week to week (for tips on doing this, see Box 2.4).

3 Seek specific advice or feedback from an expert (e.g. your research supervisor) in the skill that you're trying to master.

TYPES OF MOTIVATION

We can broadly distinguish between two types of motives: primary (biological) and secondary (psychological). Primary motives are instinctive needs which must be satisfied in order to keep us alive. For example, hunger, thirst and a need for shelter and warmth fall into this category. Conversely, secondary motives are learned desires which, although not linked directly to our biological survival, influence our happiness and well-being. Most of us have a desire to socialise with other people, which is called affiliation motivation. We also strive to attain success in some area of our lives such as school, sport or business. This phenomenon is called achievement motivation. In practice, these two categories of needs overlap considerably in everyday life.

Consider the following situation: imagine that you are studying so diligently in the library for an imminent examination that you forget to take a lunch break. After a while, your stomach starts to rumble and you begin to feel so hungry that you find yourself thinking of food. This thought is very distracting and you feel restless. In fact, you discover that you've been staring at the page for the last few minutes, reading the same sentence in your textbook over and over again (a signal that you have lost your concentration: see Chapter 6). At this point, you decide to take action. You walk out of the library and over to the restaurant for a snack. Unfortunately, as it's late, the restaurant is now closed. However, you suddenly remember that the university bar is open. There, you bump into some friends and have a cup of coffee and a sandwich with them. You haven't seen them for a while so there is a lot to talk about. After half an hour, you begin to feel uneasy again and you tell your friends that it's time to return to your books. Ignoring their pleas to stay for a drink, you tell them about your forthcoming examination and walk briskly back to the library. When you sit down, you feel refreshed and eager to get back to work.

In this vignette, several motives shaped your behaviour. To begin with, your departure from the library and subsequent visits to the restaurant and bar were initiated in the attempt to satisfy the primary need of hunger. Once your snack was over, another motivational conflict was precipitated. Would you sit down with your friends or go back to your studies? This clash between your affiliation and achievement needs is interesting for two reasons. First, it reveals how, in many everyday situations, your behaviour can be pushed and pulled in different directions. You may have felt that you were being *pulled* by your friends into staying with them at the bar, but you also felt *pushed* back to the library simply because you wanted to do well in an examination. Clearly, on this occasion, your motivation to study outweighed your desire to socialise. But it's rarely that simple. You may find yourself sitting in the library but thinking about the fun that you're missing in the bar. This 'fear of missing out' (FOMO) is a common distraction among students and one that I will discuss in Chapter 6. Of course, this conflict (*should I stay or should I go?*) can be reduced by learning to associate certain *places* with study – a strategy I'll return to later in the chapter.

There is a second reason why this conflict between motives is instructive. It shows us that, when two motives clash, a good solution may be to defer the satisfaction of one of them. This ability to defer gratification has major implications for success in life (see Box 2.3).

Box 2.3 How good are you at resisting temptation? The marshmallow challenge

---

The marshmallow challenge (see Mischel, 2014) has been hailed as an ingenious, if controversial, way of assessing people's self-control in the face of temptations. In the original studies, an experimenter offered four-year-old children a choice between two enticing treats – a single marshmallow that they could eat immediately or two marshmallows that they could eat if they could wait for 15 minutes while the experimenter left the room. Results showed that most of the children found it extremely difficult to wait for the larger reward. What intrigued Mischel and his research team was the discovery, 14 years later, that the children who had been able to delay gratification by holding out for the extra marshmallow were more likely to persist on difficult tasks as adolescents, to achieve more academic success and to cope better with frustration and stress than were their more easily-tempted counterparts (Mischel, Shoda, & Rodriguez, 1989). Subsequent studies indicated that the 'delayers' (strong self-control) fared better in life than did the 'instant gratifiers' (weak self-control) (Mischel, 2014). Not surprisingly, the marshmallow challenge continues to attract scientific attention (e.g. Doebel & Munakata, 2018) and popular debate (Resnick, 2018).

The fact that you know that you can meet your friends again means that you can delay gratification of your need to affiliate with other people – and, as Box 2.3 shows, that self-control skill is a major asset in life. Of course, the realisation that your examination is imminent and important should convince you to increase the priority of studying right now. In summary, our motivation *to do anything* is complex and influenced by a rich kaleidoscope of internal and external factors. Let us explore some of these factors now.

SOURCES OF MOTIVATION: INTRINSIC AND EXTRINSIC

As I explained in Box 2.1 (p. 16), our motivation can come from either 'intrinsic' (internal) or 'extrinsic' (external) factors – or, sometimes, from a mixture of them. Intrinsic motivation (or push) is usually characterized by a relentless curiosity, a sense of joyful adventure in mastering new skills, and, above all, a desire to pursue an activity *for its own sake* rather than for any obvious external rewards it might yield. Phil Taylor, the former darts player who won a record 16 world championships, once revealed, 'I love everything about my job – getting up every morning, practising and dedicating myself; I always try to be better' (Moran & Toner, 2017, p. 51). Interestingly, research shows that intrinsic motivation is associated with improvements in learning, performance and psychological well-being as well as with the release of dopamine, a neurotransmitter that regulates reward pathways in the brain (Di Domenico & Ryan, 2017).

Perhaps not surprisingly, intrinsic motivation provides the impetus for excellence in any field. For example, Sir Edmund Hillary, who, along with Nepalese Sherpa, Tensing Norgay, conquered Mount Everest in 1953, claimed that 'Nobody climbs mountains for scientific reasons . . . you really climb *for the hell of it*' (italics mine; cited in Plush, 2016).

In contrast, extrinsic motivation (or pull) refers to a desire to do something mainly because it provides certain rewarding consequences. For example, some students regard a degree purely and simply as a means to an end. What motivates them in university is not the intrinsic challenge of acquiring new knowledge and skills but the prospect of getting a well-paid job after graduation.

INCREASING YOUR MOTIVATION

As I mentioned earlier, there are at least three practical ways of increasing your motivation.

1 You can use self-administered rewards to increase your likelihood of studying.

2 You can motivate yourself to study by using evidence-based, goal-setting techniques.

3 You can boost your chances of studying effectively by redesigning your learning environment and by changing your study routines.

Using rewards to strengthen your behaviour: The power of positive reinforcement

In the late 1890s, an American psychologist called Edward Lee Thorndike conducted a series of experiments in which he studied the problem-solving behaviour of captive cats. In particular, he investigated how they tried to escape from cages by locating special levers which, when pressed, would open the doors of the cages and lead them to a reward of food. Thorndike discovered that rewards changed the initially random behaviour of the cats in a significant way. When the cats who had managed to escape from their cages were put back into them, they quickly searched for the release mechanism that had worked previously. This finding led Thorndike to conclude that any behaviour that leads to a satisfying state of affairs is likely to occur again – whereas any behaviour that leads to an annoying state of affairs is less likely to occur again (Gazzaniga, 2018). This principle is known as the '**law of effect**'.

Influenced by Thorndike's experiments, another famous psychologist called B. F. Skinner delved deeper into the way in which rewards and punishments influence our behaviour. In particular, he showed that, while positive reinforcers tend to strengthen associated behaviour, punishment tends to dampen behaviour. Thus, tangible rewards such as food or intangible rewards like compliments are better motivators than receiving a low grade or criticism from a teacher. How can you apply this principle of reinforcement to increase your motivation to study? The answer is: by *rewarding yourself* for successful study behaviour.

A key principle of learning theory is the idea that activities that are followed by rewards gradually tend to become rewarding *in themselves*. In other words, if you learn to associate studying with pleasurable consequences, then, over time, studying will become an enjoyable activity in its own right. To apply this principle, try giving yourself specific rewards for accomplishing planned study goals. After summarising a designated chapter in your textbook, you could take a coffee break or go on a walk. Of course, for this system to work, you must make sure to reward yourself only for the 'right' actions – those that help you to achieve your study targets – otherwise you may inadvertently strengthen undesirable behaviour and slipshod work habits. I've known students who take breaks as soon as they decide to study. Unfortunately, by doing this, they're rewarding themselves for the *very thought* of studying – not for actually doing it! Also, if you take a break every time you encounter a difficult topic in your studies (the 'I'll get back to that later' delusion!), then you're rewarding yourself for avoiding study – not for persisting with it. Remember the rule: reward yourself for work done – not for work avoided.

Before I finish this section, I'd like to explain another practical benefit of rewards. The fact that they increase motivation means that you don't have to be *initially* interested in something in order to study it thoroughly. By breaking your assignment into smaller parts and rewarding yourself for mastering each of these stepping stones, you can learn to motivate yourself indefinitely, whether or not you find the material interesting. Having discussed the power of self-administered rewards, how else can you increase your motivation to study? The answer lies in a technique called goal-setting.

Increasing your motivation through goal-setting: Study SMARTer, not harder

Reading without a question in mind is like driving to an unfamiliar destination without a map. The engine of your car is working perfectly – but you won't get to your journey's end. By analogy, effective motivation requires *direction* as well as drive and such motivation can be enhanced by a technique called goal-setting.

A goal is a target or objective that we strive to attain such as passing an exam or submitting an assignment on time. Accordingly, goal-setting is the process by which we set targets for ourselves, but some types of goals are better motivators than others. Research shows that goals that are *specific* and *under your control* tend to elicit greater effort and persistence than do more general targets. That is, studying Chapter 6 of your textbook is better than just browsing aimlessly through the book, and devising 2–3 study questions before you read this chapter is better again. To learn more about effective goal-setting, please see Box 2.4.

Box 2.4 Principles of goal-setting

To be effective, goal-setting should follow certain principles. These principles are best explained by using the acronym SMART (see Moran & Toner, 2017, for more details). Each letter of this acronym stands for a different feature of an effective goal.

S = Specific
The clearer and more specific your goal is, the more likely you are to achieve it. For example, a goal such as 'I want to make notes on Chapter 8 of my chemistry textbook tonight between 7 p.m. and 8 p.m.' is more motivating than 'I may do some chemistry later if I have time.'

M = Measurable
If you cannot measure your progress towards your goal, then you will quickly lose interest in it. So, keep a record of your progress. For example, if you're drafting a paper on a computer, you could record the number of words you've written every night just to remind yourself that you're making steady progress on the task.

A = Action-related
Unless you identify a number of action steps for each of your study goals (tasks which are under your control and which take you a step nearer to your goal), you may feel confused about what to do next. After each lecture you attend, ask yourself what particular books you can look up in the library to learn more about the material covered in class.

R = Realistic
Your study goals should be realistic and achievable. Therefore, it's important to discuss the feasibility of your goals with relevant academic staff, especially when you are working relatively independently of your supervisor.

T = Time-based

Have you ever noticed that most people do not begin jobs until a deadline approaches? Clearly, time pressure creates a sense of urgency that motivates us. To avoid panic, set a calendar reminder on your phone and work backwards from the required submission date to the present date. For example, tell yourself, 'In order to submit the assignment by the end of next month, I'll have to have it written by the middle of the month, which means I'll have to do the background research for it by next week'.

In general, goal-setting works best when you work systematically through each of the following steps.

Step 1: Identify your goals

Write down a list of *three study goals*. These goals should be under your control and as specific as possible. Write them down as promises to yourself. For example, 'Today, between 7 p.m. and 7.50 p.m., I'm going to look for an answer to the following question . . .'.

Step 2: Consider a time scale

Classify your goals into three columns depending on the time frame involved: long-term (for the end of the year), intermediate (for the end of the semester) and short-term (for this week).

Step 3: Break the goal into action steps

Next, break up each of your goals into specific action steps. For example, if one of your goals were 'to evaluate the main themes of the novel *Pride and Prejudice* by the end of next week', then obvious action steps would be to obtain and read the novel and to consult the library for critical commentaries on this novel.

Step 4: Review your progress

To maximise benefit from goal-setting, you must build a review process into your work. One way to do this is to use some time at the end of every week (perhaps even half an hour) in order to check how far away you are from achieving your goals for that week.

Step 5: Revise your goals if necessary

Flexibility is a key feature of the goal-setting cycle. Be prepared to revise your goals if you are pressed for time.

Organising your environment and your routines

Learning is not only something that happens in your head. It also involves a change in your *behaviour*. In short, learning involves *doing* things better as well as expanding your knowledge-base. In this section, I'll provide some practical tips on how to develop the behavioural habit of learning efficiently. As we'll see, this task involves at least five steps.

1   Find a quiet location that you can transform into your own personal work environment – your mental gym.

2   Establish a regular study period throughout the week.

3   As I explained in Chapter 1, you must have a specific question in mind – otherwise you will end up daydreaming (see also Chapter 6).

4   Find out which rewards will sustain your motivation to study.

5   Learn how to *finish* a study session by leaving your work in such a way that it entices you back to it again the next time you wish to study.

Chapter 3 extends this analysis of learning habits by explaining how you can manage your study time as efficiently as possible.

Find a quiet place to study

If you want to develop an effective learning habit, you have to find a place in which to study – one that doesn't have social media and emails clamouring for your attention. Research shows that repeatedly switching attention between competing tasks disrupts your learning (Putnam et al., 2016). Similarly, constantly varying the location of your study is like trying to start your car with a different set of keys each time. Just as only one key fits your ignition, so also will only *one place* be associated in your mind with effective study.

What are the requirements of this place? The ideal study should have the following characteristics: adequate space (so that you can sit comfortably at your desk or table); a clear work-top which is sufficiently large to allow you to spread out the books and notes that you are currently working on; a comfortable, straight-backed chair; storage space or shelving near the desk; natural light, where possible; and, of course, plenty of peace and quiet. In summary, find a warm, quiet, reasonably spacious, well-illuminated and distraction-free place in which to study.

If you intend to work at home, then you should make sure that you have a desk or table, a straight-backed chair, a good lamp and plenty of pens and paper at hand. By studying in this place regularly, you will condition yourself to work in it. As a result of this conditioning, you will find that you can learn to concentrate as soon as you sit down at your desk or table.

Although most quiet, well-lit locations make suitable places of study, a word of caution should be offered about trying to study in bed or while slouched on a sofa. The problem with these locations or postures is that they are passive, relaxing and likely to encourage you to daydream. Unfortunately, falling asleep over your textbooks is not restricted to your home – it's a habit that you may witness in the library too! If you plan to study in the library, choose an isolated location far away from the stairs or door, otherwise you will be tempted to interrupt your own studies by glancing repeatedly at people who pass by.

Regardless of its location, your study environment should have sufficient desk space available to enable you to spread your books, notes and computer out in front of you. Also, when you sit down to study, you need to have your pens, paper and all relevant books or notes within easy reach. If you have to get up repeatedly to look for your study material, you're creating distractions for yourself. Also, keep your phone on silent while you study and put it out of sight.

How to study in noisy environments

So far, I've indicated some factors that characterise ideal study environments. But what if you can't find one? What happens if you have to study in crowded libraries or in noisy houses? Also, is it possible to do any constructive work while you commute to and from university?

There are two main strategies for getting the most out of a distracting study environment. First, you have to prepare properly. This involves reducing your books and notes to a bare minimum so that your mind can focus on only one academic task at a time. Second, try to be as active as possible in such environments by taking notes carefully, checking the accuracy of what you have written. This advice about coping with distractions raises an important practical question for many students: does background music affect the effectiveness of your study? To find out, read Box 2.5.

Box 2.5 Can you study effectively while listening to background music?

Is it possible to study effectively while listening to background music? No – at least, not if you want to do well in exams, according to a psychological principle called the 'state dependency of learning' (Goldstein, 2011). Briefly, this principle suggests that one of the best ways for you to recall information when tested is to re-create the conditions under which the original learning occurred. The closer the resemblance between the learning and testing environments becomes, the greater are your chances of recalling the information accurately. This principle explains why police authorities reconstruct crime scenes on television. They want to cue the memories of eyewitnesses for details that may have been forgotten until the original learning situation (crime scene) was simulated.

Interestingly, this principle applies to psychological states as well as to physical environments. For example, when you are feeling down, you are more likely to recall bleak experiences from the past than when you're feeling happy. That's why people can't easily snap out of a depressed mood. How does this principle apply to studying while listening to background music? Well, it suggests that although background music may not affect what goes into your mind (the 'encoding' stage of remembering; see Chapter 8), it will affect the conditions under which it comes to mind (the retrieval stage). Therefore, as exams test your memory in largely silent conditions, it's best to study for them in silence.

Establish a regular study time

There are lots of patterns in your life. For example, you probably go to bed at around the same time on most week nights and, as likely as not, you tend to sit in the same place from lecture to lecture. Given such habitual behaviour, wouldn't it make life easier if you had a regular study schedule during the week as well? Ideally, you should try to study in the same place at the same time every day or evening. It may help to visualise this study period as 'red traffic light time' that gives you the signal to stop all other activities while you study. Conversely, other periods of the day could be pictured as 'green traffic light time' during which you can socialise, get some exercise or do other mundane chores. Some practical tips on time management are provided in Chapter 3.

Have a specific question in mind

In Chapter 1, I explained that asking questions transforms aimless reading into purposeful study. So, make sure to write down 2–3 specific questions before you begin your reading.

Start with a simple 'lead in' task

To overcome your mind's initial reluctance to engage in studying, make a start with a simple lead-in task, such as flicking through the pages of a chapter to get an overview of what it's about. This simple technique should boost your motivation. And remember the Irish saying: '*Tosach maith, leath na h-oibre!*' (Irish proverb: 'A good start is half the battle'; see also Moran & O'Connell, 2006).

Finish your study by preparing for the next time and giving yourself a reward

Finish your study by clearing your desk briefly and leaving a note to yourself about the question you're going to tackle when you resume. That way, you're making your work environment as inviting as possible for your next study session. Also, it's very important to give yourself a little reward for completing a study session.

Unfortunately, most students are so anxious to finish studying that they leave their books and notes in a state of disarray. Obviously, such a sight is very demoralising when you have to study that material again. It is a good idea to spend the last 2–3 minutes of your study schedule tidying your books and notes and writing down some specific study questions that need to be addressed when you resume your work.

SUMMARY

Getting down to study is always difficult because deliberate learning is hard work. Even when you conquer your inertia, a host of displacement activities such as taking a break or checking social media may seem irresistible. Therefore, the purpose of this chapter was to explore what motivation is, where it comes from and how to harness it properly in order to develop an efficient habit of learning. As I explained, the term motivation refers to all those factors that initiate, direct and sustain your behaviour.

To begin with, I helped you to clarify your motives for coming to university. As you probably discovered, these motives tend to reflect a blend of external and internal factors (e.g. other people's expectations versus a desire to improve your education).

Although these types of factors often overlap, intrinsic motivation is usually more important than external influences in the long run as it encourages energy and persistence in times of difficulty. But effective study requires *direction* as well as energy.

In the remainder of the chapter, I explained three practical motivational techniques which can improve the quality of your learning.

I showed you how to use rewards to strengthen your study behaviour. A key principle here is that activities that are followed by rewarding consequences tend to become rewarding in themselves.

Using goal-setting principles, I explained how to study SMARTer rather than harder. To explain, the acronym SMART represents the first letters of the qualities that study goals should have if they are to elicit optimal motivation. These qualities are specific, measurable, action-related, realistic and time-based.

I explained how a reorganisation of your study environment and behavioural routines can improve the quality of your learning. This section also included a discussion of the effects of background music on studying. As I explained, such music does not normally affect the information that goes *into* your mind – but it can determine the circumstances under which it comes *out* of your mind (i.e. when you attempt to recall it). Therefore, you should study in silence simply because you will be tested under silent conditions in the exam hall.

MÁ CHAILLEAN TÚ UAIR AR MAIDIN, BEIDH TÚ Á TÓRAIOCHT I RITH AN LAE.

Irish proverb:
*'If you lose an hour in the morning,
you will look for it all day.'*

Chapter 3

Managing Your Study Time Effectively

How Much? How Often? For How Long?

INTRODUCTION

Many students believe that the longer they spend poring over their books, notes or computer screens, the more successful they'll be in university. Unfortunately, it's not that simple for two main reasons. You can sit in front of your books for hours on end and yet learn very little because, as I explained in Chapter 1, reading and studying are different mental processes (see also Chapter 6). 'Hours spent in a study situation' is not a good measure of efficient learning. The only valid index of successful study is whether or not you obtained specific answers to your specific study questions. In addition, research shows that it is the *quality* rather than the quantity of your study that determines the richness and durability of your learning (Putnam et al., 2016). For example, one hour spent looking for answers to questions (see Chapter 5) is more beneficial to your learning than three hours spent in aimless reading or in passive transcription from a textbook while your mind is miles away. For these reasons, it's very important to manage your study time efficiently in university. Therefore, the purpose of the present chapter is to give you some practical tips on this skill.

This chapter is organised as follows:
....
- ➤ I'll help you to assess your current use of study time.
- ➤ I'll explore the main time-wasters that may hamper your studies and I will suggest some ways of overcoming them.

➤ I'll explain some practical time-management techniques ranging from daily goal-setting to making effective timetables. This section will also feature a discussion of the merits of 'spaced' versus 'massed' learning (the latter being known more popularly as 'cramming').

•••

ASSESSING YOUR USE OF STUDY TIME

How do you spend your time in university on a typical day during term? In order to answer this question, please complete the activity diary in Box 3.1.

Box 3.1 My activity diary: Charting my use of time

Pick a recent day during term (e.g. yesterday). Fill in brief details of your time log under the two columns shown: what academic activity you engaged in (e.g. attending a lecture; looking for a book in the library) and whether or not this activity was planned or spontaneous.

Time period	The day in question	
	Academic activity	Planned or spontaneous?
09.30–10.30		
10.30–11.30		
11.30–12.30		
14.00–15.00		
15.00–16.00		
16.00–17.00		
19.00–20.00		
20.00–21.00		

Do you spot any trend with regard to your use of study time for the day in question? Were the majority of your academic activities planned or unplanned on that day? By examining the pattern of your activity diary, you may discover that you have a lot more time available for private study than you realised. Also, you may discover that your learning is influenced more by accidental than by deliberate factors (see also Chapter 1) – a typical sign that you need to cultivate some time-management skills.

Try to *impose some structure* on the syllabus so that you can identify your priorities. Then, plan to distribute your time accordingly. This can be achieved by seeking advice from your tutors and professor during their office hours about the relative importance of different topics on the course. How can you know what is important and what to focus on unless you *ask* someone? In addition, as I have explained elsewhere (see Chapters 1 and 5), you should always write down 2–3 *specific study questions* before you read a textbook.

WASTING TIME: COMMON STUDY PROBLEMS AND HOW TO OVERCOME THEM

Wasting study time means spending it unwisely on activities that you *know* to be irrelevant to your academic goals. Some of these time-wasting activities are described in the following sections – along with possible solutions.

Not knowing how or where to start

Reading without any clear idea of what you are looking for is a waste of time – so is feeling sorry for yourself because nobody has told you where to start or what to study.

Procrastination: 'I'll do it later (maybe)'

Procrastination is the habit of voluntarily postponing an important task that you intend to do – despite knowing that you'll suffer more and perform worse as a consequence. In short, it's a form of self-sabotage. Whether caused by poor time-management skills or an inability to regulate your emotions, it can be triggered by a variety of factors such as:

- Not feeling in the mood: 'I'm not in the right frame of mind to tackle that job now.'

- Tiredness: 'I just don't have the energy to tackle this task at the moment. I'll do it later.'

- Distractibility: 'I'll tidy my desk and check my emails before I begin.'

- Perfectionism: 'I don't feel ready now but I know I'll be able to do a much better job on this assignment later.'

- Self-delusion: 'I always work better under pressure.'

But remember that if something is important to you, you'll *make* time to do it *right now*. How can you overcome procrastination? See Box 3.2.

Box 3.2 Practical tips on overcoming procrastination

---

1 Don't make such a big deal of the assignment – it may not be as difficult, boring or unpleasant as you expect.

2 Break your assignment into smaller, more manageable parts to avoid being overwhelmed.

3 Reward yourself for achieving progress on each part of the task – no matter how small (e.g. by having a quick cup of coffee or listening to a favourite song).

4 Don't wait to be in the right mood: act first and your mood will follow. Seek help: ask someone else to check on your progress.

5 Keep at it! It may take a while, but you can replace your habit of procrastination with a habit of efficient work.

Task-hopping

Jumping from one study activity to another depending on your prevailing mood is a symptom of poor concentration and inefficient time management. As I shall explain in Chapter 6, **monotasking** will help you to get the most of your study time.

Missing opportunities to study as you travel to and from university

Most students dismiss the hours they spend in commuting to and from university as dead time. But travel time can be used fruitfully if you use it to glance over summary sheets that contain condensed answers to typical questions asked in exams (see also revision techniques in Chapter 10).

In summary, time-wasting activities can come in many different guises. What they have in common, however, is the fact that they divert your attention away from what is important and towards what is irrelevant. The best way to overcome them is by using a set of practical time-management techniques that are described in the next section.

TECHNIQUES FOR MANAGING YOUR STUDY TIME EFFECTIVELY

According to Butler, Grey and Hope, successful time management boils down to 'doing those things you value or those things that help you achieve your goals' (p. 178, 2018). Unfortunately, this advice assumes that you have already established your study goals and priorities. If you're like most students, you will probably drift through university without planning specific academic goals. If so, you could benefit from the following time-management techniques.

Daily goal-setting

In Chapter 2, I explained the SMART approach to goal-setting. This approach shows you how to set specific, measurable, action-related, realistic and time-based targets for your studies. SMART goal-setting is effective because immediate targets are more motivating than distant targets. Remember, if you work on what's under your control right now, the future will look after itself (see also Chapter 6).

Establish daily study priorities

Distinguish between three kinds of study tasks:

1   Jobs I *must do* today (top priority tasks such as attending lectures)

2 Jobs I *should do* today (desirable but not essential on a daily basis such as studying in the library)

3 Jobs I'd *like to do* today (inessential tasks such as reading 'around' your course).

Develop routines

Establish a routine for lecture and non-lecture days. For lecture days, ask yourself questions like: *Who is the lecturer? What course is she or he teaching? What was covered last week? What will we explore this week?*

After lectures, you could spend 2–3 minutes going through a brief after-lecture routine: *Have I attached my lecture notes to the previous lecture on this course? What specific books or articles did the lecturer mention? If I didn't note them, can I get this information from a classmate?* For non-lecture days, ask yourself what your study tasks are and make a plan for how to perform them.

DISTRIBUTED PRACTICE

People learn better if they study regularly and briefly (distributed practice) than if they study infrequently for long periods (massed practice or **cramming**).

Distributed practice has several advantages. It gives you a steady diet of success every day. Its brevity helps you to remain alert and focused over your books. Finally, it encourages the 'incubation' of ideas – thinking about things unconsciously between study sessions. This principle of distributed learning is explained in detail in Box 3.3.

Box 3.3 Spacing your study periods over time: The effects of massed versus distributed practice

---

It has long been known that the more you study something, the more likely you will be to remember it, but it was not until the late 1880s that the German psychologist Hermann Ebbinghaus discovered that the way in which we distribute our study over time influences the amount of learning that occurs. He concluded that 'with any considerable number of repetitions, a suitable distribution of them over a space of time is decidedly more advantageous than the massing of them at a single time'

(Ebbinghaus, 1885/1964, p. 89). In other words, it's better to space out your learning over time (distributed practice) than it is to cram it all into one intense study period (massed practice).

Research shows that spacing your learning in this way doesn't take any longer than cramming – but is much more effective in promoting long-term learning (Putnam et al., 2016). For example, information acquired though cramming tends to be forgotten quickly (Bjork & Bjork, 2011). Remarkably, the inefficiency of cramming was recognized well over a century ago by James (1890) who observed that 'things learned in a few hours, on one occasion, for one purpose, cannot possibly have formed many associations with other things in the mind. Speedy oblivion is the almost inevitable fate of all that is committed to memory in this simple way ... Whereas on the contrary, the same information taken in gradually, day after day, recurring in different contexts ... and repeatedly reflected on, grow into a fabric, lie open to so many paths of approach, that they remain as permanent possessions' (Vol. 1, p. 663).

Why does distributed practice work so well? Several possible explanations exist. For example, the more regularly you study something, the richer and more elaborate your understanding of it becomes. Another possibility is that the more opportunities you get to expand or augment your learning, the more durable it becomes.

By contrast, the problem with cramming is that it taxes your concentration and induces fatigue. Worse still, cramming before examinations can cause exam blank in which students experience the awful feeling of knowing that they know something but are unable to recall it at that moment. In summary, it's better to study briefly and regularly than to try to cram information into your brain at the last minute.

HOW MUCH STUDY? FOR HOW LONG?

What's the golden rule on optimising study amount and study duration? Unfortunately, to paraphrase George Bernard Shaw, 'The golden rule is that there is no golden rule!' As courses vary widely in their demands, and as students differ so much in their interests and abilities, it's impossible to offer significant conclusions about the optimal amount or duration of study required for academic success. However, you should follow any study recommendations provided by your professors in the module description.

If none is available, try scheduling at least *two hours of private study for each hour of formal lectures* on your timetable as a good rule of thumb. This two-hour period should be used as follows:

- To maximise your concentration, study in blocks of 40–50 minutes.

- Specify at least one study question per block.

- After two hours, spend five minutes reviewing what you learned (see principle of 'overlearning' in Chapter 8).

- Write down any persistent distractions on a 'distraction list' which you can deal with after your study session.

- Look for opportunities of 5–10 minutes duration each day (e.g. between lectures, while waiting for a friend, while travelling in a bus or train) to quickly scan your 'summary sheets' (see Chapter 10).

- Use spare moments to revise or to plan. There is bound to be free time even in the busiest of academic time-tables. For example, you might find that you have an hour to spend in between scheduled lectures. In this case, you could either review what you learned in the previous lecture or check your progress on your daily job list.

REVIEW THE TIME YOU SPEND ON DIFFERENT SUBJECTS AND COURSES

Allocating study time equally to all your subjects or courses is a major challenge for students. For one thing, you may be far more interested in one topic than another. Accordingly, you will tend to spend more time on it than on other topics.

In addition, the unstructured nature of university life means that advice on time management is difficult to obtain. But perhaps a simple adjustment to your daily routine may help. You should develop the habit of spending ten minutes each night in reviewing what you did on each of your major subject areas during that day. Even if this review shows that you did nothing in a particular area, you have succeeded in alerting yourself to the danger of neglecting this area on your course.

SCHEDULE DIFFERENT JOBS
FOR DIFFERENT TIMES

It is a good idea to schedule different types of study tasks for different times of the day. Although students vary in their preferred learning times (some people are 'night owls' whereas others are 'morning larks'), research suggests that jobs that require intense concentration (e.g. revising for an exam or writing a term paper) should be undertaken during uninterrupted times early in the morning. The big advantage of doing your most demanding work at this time is captured by the maxim 'If you do it early, it's done sooner'. As the day progresses, lots of other jobs will clamour for your attention. Therefore, it is important to begin your studies as early as possible to avoid being gridlocked by having too many jobs to do at the one time.

DISTINGUISH BETWEEN URGENT
AND IMPORTANT TASKS

Experts on time management make a distinction between two kinds of tasks. On the one hand, urgent tasks have to be completed by a certain deadline (e.g. to submit a paper as part of your coursework). On the other hand, important tasks are those that have a clear and specific relevance to your personal study-goals. For example, if you are interested in a particular career such as marketing, then it may be important for you to arrange work experience for the summer in the marketing department of a company at home or abroad. Planning, obtaining relevant information and making personal contacts in this field are important, but not necessarily urgent goals. And yet, these activities are often neglected in our haste to perform more urgent jobs.

Using this distinction between different types of tasks, we can see that the greatest waste of time occurs when we are preoccupied by activities that are neither important nor urgent (e.g. colour coding your lecture notes). By contrast, study tasks that demand your immediate action are those that are both urgent and important (e.g. planning an academic assignment; revising for an exam). In order to avoid unnecessary stress, try to arrange your daily time-table to maximise the time you spend in performing *important* rather than *urgent* jobs.

Using the traffic light analogy that I referred to in the last chapter, you should interpret the early part of the morning as 'red traffic light time' that gives you the signal to stop all other activities while you study. Meanwhile, routine tasks that require less mental effort (such as borrowing books from the library) may be performed later in the day.

MAKE AN EFFECTIVE TIMETABLE: PRACTICAL TIPS

How much study time do you have available each week? Make out a timetable for a typical week and assess *realistically* how many hours of private study time are available to you, taking into account other demands on your time that arise from such activities as a part-time job, commuting to university, meal times, coffee breaks, exercise activities, hobbies and sports, social life, leisure periods, time to perform routine chores and, of course, sleep time. When you have established how many study hours are available to you, identify your specific study goals (see Chapter 2). Write down your study tasks under three headings:

- Short-term daily or weekly goals (e.g. to read the chapter in a textbook that was referred to in a lecture today)

- Intermediate-term goals (e.g. to conduct library research for an essay that has to be submitted by the end of this term or semester)

- Long-term goals (e.g. to perform as well as possible in end-of-year examinations).

Always specify a starting time and a finishing time for your study session. Without a finishing time, your mind will begin to wander. Before you begin to study, write down 2–3 specific study questions (see Chapter 5). As the phrase goes, 'Ink them, don't just think them.' For each of these study goals, list 2–3 relevant actions that you can take that will bring you one step nearer to your goal – the more specific your action steps, the better. Next, specify a brief time frame for each step (e.g. '10.00–10.50. Go to the library to obtain key references mentioned in class today').

Try to arrange your study time in blocks of 2–3 hours, devoting approximately 50 minutes each to a different study question (see advice on summarising skills in Chapter 5). At the end of each 50-minute study period, you should take a 3–5 minute break. After you have finished a 2–3 hour block, spend 5–10 minutes reviewing what you have learned. Specifically, you should ask yourself what information you have acquired and how it relates to what you already know. Glance over your summary sheets (see Chapter 5) as you review your progress.

Try to make sure that the academic tasks that require the greatest mental work or concentration are scheduled for your best times each day: those periods when you feel most energetic and alert.

If your timetable is not helping you to achieve progress, arrange an appointment to meet your academic tutor or a staff member and seek advice from her or him on how best to achieve your goal. When arranging to meet professors in your department or school, please note their official 'office hours' (the times during which they're available to meet students). If these times do not suit you, email the relevant professors to seek a formal appointment with them to discuss your queries.

As I mentioned earlier, a good rule of thumb is to schedule at least two hours of private study for every formal lecture hour on your timetable. Additional time will have to be devoted to other assignments such as practicals (e.g. drawing in Engineering).

TAKE REGULAR EXERCISE: MOVING YOUR BODY BOOSTS YOUR BRAIN

It is well known that physical activity is as good for your mind as it is for your body. Thus, the old Latin phrase *solvitur ambuladno* ('it is solved by walking') rings true. More precisely, taking regular aerobic exercise that gets your heart pumping and your body sweating, such as vigorous walking, cycling, swimming, playing competitive sport or working out in the gym improves brain function, sharpens your mental processes and boosts mental health. Research shows that the **hippocampus** grows as a function of increased physical fitness (Erickson et al., 2011). Regular exercise also improves concentration (de Sousa et al., 2018), memory (Heisz,

Clark, Bonin, Michalski, Becker & Fahnestock, 2017) and psychological well-being (Mandolesi et al., 2018). These remarkable effects are probably due to the fact that exercise not only stimulates blood flow to the brain but also promotes 'neurogenesis' or the birth of new brain cells. As a general rule, try to take at least 30 minutes of brisk physical activity every day. If you can't find the time for 30 minutes of exercise at one go, then three 10-minute bouts of high-intensity physical activity is equally beneficial. The lesson is clear: make regular physical activity part of your lifestyle.

SUMMARY

Without self-discipline, the free time that is available in university can easily become wasted time. This chapter provided some practical tips designed to increase the efficiency of your study time. I began by asking you to complete a time log of your study activities for a given day. Then I reviewed some problems which could serve as potential time-wasters for students. In particular, three obstacles to efficient study were analysed. These factors included:

- Not knowing how or where to start your work

- Engaging in procrastination

- Indulging in task-hopping (i.e. flitting from one activity to another depending on your prevailing mood)

- Missing opportunities to study as you travel to and from university.

In an effort to combat these problems, I presented a range of practical time-management techniques. Included here was advice on:

- daily goal-setting

- establishing study priorities and routines

- the need for brief but regular learning sessions

- scheduling your academic tasks to coincide with periods of maximum alertness

- the distinction between urgent and important jobs.

Tips on making effective timetables as well as on the benefits of regular exercise were also provided.

NOT ALL HIS CLASS ATTEND HIS LECTURES. OF THOSE WHO ATTEND, ONLY HALF LISTEN TO WHAT HE SAYS. OF THOSE WHO ATTEND AND LISTEN, ONLY HALF UNDERSTAND. OF THOSE WHO ATTEND, AND LISTEN, AND UNDERSTAND, ONLY HALF REMEMBER. OF THOSE WHO ATTEND AND LISTEN AND UNDERSTAND AND REMEMBER, ONLY HALF AGREE.

Former President of Yale University (1986)

with contributions from Helen O'Shea

Chapter 4

Learning from Lectures and Virtual Learning Environments

Practical Tips

INTRODUCTION

Despite occasional concerns about its efficacy, the formal lecture has been the most popular teaching method in university education for over 900 years (Freeman et al., 2014). In the modern version of this venerable method, a professor or lecturer (I'll use those terms interchangeably) delivers a presentation on a specific topic for about 50 minutes, typically supported by multimedia. During this period of time, attending students are encouraged to take relevant notes on the material presented. Therefore, learning from lectures depends greatly on efficient note-taking – a complex mental activity that interweaves listening skills (comprehension) and writing skills (production) (Piolat, Olive, & Kellogg, 2004).

As it's unlikely that you received any training in this cognitive skill at school (see Box 1.5, p. 12), note-taking raises a number of practical questions. For example, should you try to record everything that your professor says in class using your phone or computer – assuming that you've received permission to do so? If not, is it better to type your notes on a laptop or tablet or write them in longhand? Also, how do you know which points to note and which ones to ignore?

If you've struggled with such questions, don't despair. Many students find it difficult to adjust to lecture-based teaching systems in university. One reason for this problem is that professors tend to speak much faster than you can write and so your limited capacity working memory (see Chapters 5 and 8) is easily overwhelmed by rapidly-delivered information. The good news, however, is that you won't have to transcribe everything that you hear and see in class because lecture notes are normally available through your university's '**virtual learning environment**' (VLE; see later in this chapter), which is a web-based learning management system that enables professors and students to interact using digital tools and activities. Examples of VLEs include Blackboard, Moodle and Brightspace. The purpose of this chapter, therefore, is to give you some practical tips on learning from lectures and on getting the most out of your experience of VLEs. Before we begin, let's explore what makes a good note-taker.

Most students develop a distinctive note-taking style. For example, you may act like a sponge in class, trying to mop up everything that your professor says or shows you. Unfortunately, as you'll discover, this approach is too passive and indiscriminate to boost your learning. Alternatively, you may see yourself as a shrewd prospector, sifting lecture content for interesting ideas or nuggets of gold. Either way, one thing is certain: effective note-taking requires active listening – *thinking along with* your professors to such an extent that you can 'see' where the lecture is going. This interactive approach encourages you to develop a deep understanding of lecture content because you're trying to link new material with what you already know (see 'elaborative rehearsal' in Chapter 8). By contrast, poor note-takers are so preoccupied with indiscriminate absorption of every single word uttered in class that they sacrifice *understanding* the material in favour of verbatim recording. Interestingly, active engagement is as crucial to learning from VLEs as it is to learning from lectures. As I'll explain later, research on students' experience of VLEs suggests that, in order to make the most of these digital tools for collaborative learning, you'll need to go beyond using them for logistical purposes such as downloading notes and articles and, instead, embrace their potential for *interactivity*. The key to this interactivity is in communicating and collaborating as often as possible with other students and your professors on module-related learning tasks (Raftery, 2018).

Of course, you'll also have access to a host of other digital learning resources provided by the academic schools and departments in your university such as podcasts, wikis and blogs (see advice in Cottrell & Morris, 2012). Although each of these platforms has its own unique strengths, VLEs are particularly important because they provide the 'core infrastructure' for your digital learning experiences in university (Raftery & Risquez, 2018). Accordingly, I'll give you some practical tips on getting the most out of VLEs later in this chapter. Continuing this theme of digital learning, I'll mention the potential benefits of using augmented reality and virtual reality in your studies. The chapter concludes with a checklist of questions that will help you to critically evaluate online sources of information when conducting your research (see also Chapter 9).

This chapter is organised as follows:

➤ I'ill consider the cognitive challenge of learning from lectures. This task requires you to learn how to think and write simultaneously.

➤ I'll consider five common barriers to learning from lectures and give you practical tips on how to overcome them.

➤ I'll give you practical tips on what to do before, during and after your lectures to improve your learning.

➤ I'll highlight the importance of VLEs for digital learning and explore some of the advantages of VLEs over social media.

➤ I'll give you some 'dos and don'ts' when engaging in academic online communication.

➤ I'll give you practical tips on getting the most out of VLEs.

➤ I'll give you a checklist of questions to help you to critically evaluate online information.

THE COGNITIVE CHALLENGE OF LEARNING FROM LECTURES

Lectures have three key strengths as teaching techniques:

1 They provide an efficient way of transmitting information to large groups of people in a relatively short duration.

2 The flexibility of their format ensures that they can be used for an impressive range of educational purposes. For example,

a lecture can provide a frame of reference for a new topic, it can help to disseminate recent advances in an existing body of knowledge, and it can encourage critical evaluation of a given idea or approach.

3   The drama and immediacy of a well-crafted lecture can inspire audiences in emotional ways. Indeed, long after you've graduated, you'll still vividly remember those professors whose enthusiasm and passion for their subject was both palpable and contagious.

Unfortunately, like all teaching tools, lectures have some disadvantages. For example, you may struggle to maintain your concentration during a 50-minute presentation as the sheer volume of material covered may overwhelm your limited attention span. So, would shortening the duration of a lecture reduce the danger of cognitive overload?

This approach has been adopted by TED talks (Technology, Entertainment and Design), the popular online video resource. Intriguingly, these talks cannot exceed 18 minutes, no matter who the speaker is. According to Chris Anderson, TED curator, this duration is short enough to hold people's attention but long enough to enable speakers to make their point effectively (Gallo, 2014). Does scientific evidence support the claim that students' attention span in lectures is as short as 10 to 15 minutes (Davis, 1993)? No – according to Bradbury (2016) and Wilson & Korn (2007), most studies in this field have failed to take account of major individual differences between students' interest and motivation. It seems that attention span in lectures is easily underestimated.

A second possible weakness of lectures concerns the quality of their delivery. Historically, professors have been recruited more for their *research* productivity than for their ability to teach effectively. Therefore, although they know a lot about their subject, professors are not always skilful presenters. Some of them are so passionate about their subject that they race through their lectures at breakneck speed – making it difficult for you to take notes. This raises the challenge of effective listening.

Superficially, the task of listening to a lecture seems no different from participating in an everyday conversation. You have to decode what someone says to you as they utter between 100–200 words per minute. However, paying attention to a lecture differs significantly from other forms of listening. To begin with, it involves taking notes – not something that occurs in everyday conversational exchanges. Furthermore, formal lectures are not as interactive as conversations, where participants switch regularly between the roles of speaker and listener.

There is a way to remain focused at lectures: it involves *asking yourself questions* as you listen. Questions like, 'What's the main point she or he is making?' or 'What's an example of this idea?' will help you to anticipate what the professor is likely to say next. A more technical analysis of the psychological processes involved in listening to a lecture is presented in Box 4.1.

Box 4.1 Making sense of a lecture: What cognitive processes are required?

According to Smyth, Collins, Morris and Levy (1994), the act of making sense of a lecture in a noisy, crowded theatre is a sophisticated cognitive activity involving several mental processes that work together in less than a few seconds.

- Your perceptual and word-recognition processes need to segment the stream of speech sounds that emanate from the professor's mouth.

- You have to analyse the syntactic structure of the sentences uttered by the speaker. This task involves a great deal of prediction. Determiner words like 'a' or 'the' usually indicate the beginning of a noun phrase whereas words like 'because' suggest that a new clause is about to occur in a sentence.

- At this stage, your '**phonological loop**' is pressed into action. This is the component of your working memory system that is responsible for maintaining speech sounds for about 1.5 seconds – your 'inner voice' (see Chapter 8). In order to understand a long sentence, you need to be able to store the first few words in your inner voice while you process the last few words.

- To make any sense of what the professor is saying, you have to use relevant background knowledge to comprehend the sentences being uttered.

- Finally, you need to be able summarise the most important points of the lecture in a form that you will understand later when you review your notes.

Let's now consider five common barriers to learning from lectures.

FIVE COMMON BARRIERS TO LEARNING FROM LECTURES AND HOW TO OVERCOME THEM

1. Failing to prepare for the lecture

Some students think that simply turning up for a lecture means you are learning from it. That's a myth. Research shows that active learning techniques such as glancing over your previous week's lecture notes before class will help you to 'elaborate' your understanding (i.e. to connect new information to what you already know). Similarly, if your professors make their PowerPoint slides available before lectures, why not skim through them briefly in advance? Research suggests that students learn more if they are given slides *before* class rather than after it (Putnam et al., 2016). If your professors suggest reading a specific article or book before a given lecture, do it. Successful learning requires you to think about a theory or idea many times.

2. Trying to write down everything you hear or see

You don't have to write down what a professor says or shows on screen verbatim for three good reasons:

1 Trying to record everything that they say at normal conversational speed is futile because they can speak much faster than you can write or type.

2 You can remotely access your professors' lecture notes online through your university's VLE.

3 Good lecturers understand the importance of subtle and interwoven repetition. By making the same point in various ways

using different examples, they allow you to take a breather during a class from time to time.

How exactly should you take your notes during lectures? Is the pen really mightier than the keyboard? See Box 4.2.

Box 4.2 Longhand note-taking versus laptop note-taking

Some students believe that using laptops during lectures facilitates their note-taking because they can type significantly faster than they can write. By contrast, many professors feel that multitasking with laptops (especially those with access to the internet) distracts students from relevant learning and inhibits class discussion. In an attempt to arbitrate between these rival views, Mueller & Oppenheimer (2014) evaluated the efficiency of longhand versus laptop note-taking in lectures.

Results showed that students using laptops were more inclined to take verbatim notes than students who wrote by hand. More importantly, the students who had taken notes with laptops performed worse than their longhand counterparts on subsequent tests of factual recall and conceptual understanding of the lecture material. A possible explanation of these findings is that longhand note-taking triggers 'generative' processing of lecture content (Miyatsu, Nguyen, & McDaniel, 2018). In other words, it facilitates a deeper and more elaborate processing of information than does verbatim transcription. Based on the findings of this study, it may be wise to leave your laptops out of the lecture hall!

---

3. Failing to impose a structure on what the lecturer says

Have you ever noticed that unfamiliar languages sound as if they're being spoken faster than familiar ones? This phenomenon is probably due to the fact that if we don't understand word meanings in a language, we can't impose any organisation on the stream of speech sounds that we hear. Listening to a lecture is a bit like trying to segment speech sounds: in order to understand the content, you need to impose *organisation* on what you hear. Do this by listening very carefully to opening remarks at the beginning of the lecture and the summary at the end.

4. Failing to identify signpost words from the lecturer

Good lecturers use verbal signposts to signal to their audiences that certain details of their presentation are especially important. For example, they may use phrases like 'There are three features . . .', 'In summary . . .' or 'The key point here is . . .' to tell you to note crucial points. By listening carefully for such phrases, you will be able to identify the key ideas in every lecture that you attend.

5. Indulging a wandering mind

It's almost impossible to focus solely on the present moment because our concentration system has many mental tasks to take care of, such as deciding what to focus on, scanning our environment for signs of novelty or danger, coordinating our actions and anticipating the future (see Chapter 6 for practical tips on concentration). That's why 'mind wandering', or disengaging your attention from the world around you and directing it towards your own thoughts and feelings (see Szpunar, 2017), is so prevalent during lectures. In order to prevent such daydreaming, it's helpful to think along with the professor and ask yourself questions like 'Is this information new to me?' or 'How does this fit with what I already know?'

PRACTICAL TIPS ON GETTING THE MOST OUT OF YOUR LECTURES — BEFORE, DURING AND AFTERWARDS

In order to improve your note-taking skills, you need to become a more active learner. You can do this by performing the following tasks before, during and after lectures.

Develop a pre-lecture routine

Most skilled performers, such as athletes, have developed character-istic sequences of thoughts and actions called 'routines' to help them to focus properly before executing important skills (see Moran & Toner, 2017). Routines are valuable because they take you from thinking about a skill to actually doing it. By immersing yourself in each step of your routine, you can focus on the present moment while blocking out distractions. In general, weaker students have fewer and less consistent routines than successful ones. Here are some tips for a useful pre-lecture routine.

- Arrive early. Take your seat about 3–5 minutes before the lecture begins and make sure to get a clear view of the projection screen.

- Skim though your lecture notes to find out what was covered in the previous lecture.

- Put the date and topic at the top of your page.

- Make sure that you begin your notes for each lecture on a separate page. This will help you to organise and file them properly later.

Take lecture notes selectively: More is not necessarily better

In general, adopting an active 'prospector' approach to note-taking – looking for nuggets of gold in what the professor says – is better than verbatim transcription. But remember that your lecture notes are only a means of helping you with your private study of assigned readings, not an end in themselves. Unfortunately, many students fall into the trap of believing that just because they have a neat set of lecture notes on a topic, they understand it. Ownership doesn't guarantee understanding. As Anthony Burgess (1966) once remarked, 'The possession of a book becomes a substitute for reading it.' Similarly, having a photocopy of something is no guarantee that you actually understand it (a myth called 'the seduction of reproduction'; see also Chapters 5 and 9). Don't waste time in photocopying lecture notes – summarise them instead.

By the way, there is little to be gained in transcribing your notes to make them look neater. Verbatim copying of notes is not effective but summarising and re-organising them improves understanding. One way of doing this is to look for common themes or ideas (Bjork et al., 2013; Miyatsu et al., 2018).

Organise the lecture in your mind

It is difficult to understand or remember information that lacks a structure. For example, if we can classify something we are told, then we can link the new information with what we already know. To demonstrate this principle for yourself, try the exercise in Box 4.3.

The purpose of this exercise is to show you that you can improve your note-taking skills by trying to impose some order or meaning on new information as you acquire it (see also Chapter 8).

Box 4.3 The importance of linking new information with what you already know

Understanding a lecture requires you to organise new information under headings so that you can link it to what you already know. To test your ability to do this, can you make any sense of the following information?

'The procedure is really quite simple. First you have to arrange items into different groups. Sometimes, one pile may be sufficient – but it depends on how much material has accumulated since the last operation. If you can't do the job yourself, then you may have to bring the stuff elsewhere. Otherwise, you're ready to go. But try not to do too much at the one time. A mistake at this stage could ruin one of your favourite items. Although this task may seem quite complicated at the beginning, you will soon accept it as a weekly routine. And while the job is in progress, you can do other things with your time. After it is finished, however, you will have to rearrange the items into piles and take them to the next stage of the cycle. Eventually, they will be used again and the whole process will have to be repeated' (based on Bransford & Johnson, 1972).

Most students find this passage of information incomprehensible! Why? Because the text lacks a frame of reference – a scaffolding to help you to organise it properly. If there were a heading that could help you to make sense of this passage, you would find it a lot easier to memorise. Try to guess it before turning to the end of the chapter. When you have discovered the appropriate heading, re-read the text and notice how quickly all of the words make sense to you. This happens because the heading activates your prior knowledge of the topic (see also Chapter 8).

Be curious: Ask questions in your mind before the presentation starts

Just before the professor begins the lecture, try to think of a few questions that might be covered in the presentation. Asking questions is a practical tool for making sense of things – for forging connections between new material and what you already know (see also principles of 'depth of processing' and 'elaborative rehearsal' in Chapter 8).

Divide and conquer

Try to divide lectures into three parts: the beginning (introduction); the middle (central theme and supporting details); and the end (conclusion). In the introduction, the professor usually reminds you of what she or he covered in the last class and gives a brief overview of the theme of the current lecture. Then she or he outlines details of the main evidence or arguments. Finally, the last part of a lecture is usually devoted to a review of the conclusions or the 'take home' message. Take careful notes at the beginning and the end of the lecture – but be selective about the notes that you take during the middle as this information can usually be obtained from the readings assigned to the lecture.

In the first few minutes of any class the lecturer tends to 'set the scene' for the talk using such strategies as asking rhetorical questions, giving a brief overview of what she or he intends to cover or by trying to link what is about to be discussed with what was covered in the previous lecture. These opening remarks are vital to your learning because they establish 'advance organisers' which will increase your understanding of, and **memory** for, what is about to be discussed. Unfortunately, many students miss out on these key points because they arrive late, look around for where their friends are sitting or make noise by shuffling their bags or notes. These distractions prevent you from being properly 'tuned in' to the class. Indeed, a failure to pay attention to the initial few moments of a presentation may explain why students lose their concentration so easily during class. Pay attention to the early part of a message because understanding the specific theme or purpose of the lecture is half the battle – you can look up the precise details or supporting evidence after class in the prescribed textbook for the course.

The main part of a lecture is usually devoted to an explanation of details such as historical issues, theories, principles or research findings. Because of the amount of material covered, it may be difficult to take notes on everything that is presented to you. Try to make sure that you write down key names and dates, ideas or headings, especially if the lecturer gives some reason as to why these details are particularly important.

The last few minutes of a lecture are vital because they usually contain the lecturer's summary of relevant conclusions. Unfortunately, many students miss these points for two main reasons. The professor may have stopped showing new slides, thereby conveying the false impression that the lecture is over. Additionally, the student may be preparing for her or his next class and may have packed hastily for a quick getaway.

Pay special attention to professors' signpost words

As I explained earlier, effective listening is an active process in which one person tries to make sense of, and anticipate, what the other is saying. Using active listening principles, here are some tips on improving your listening in class.

- Pay special attention to any signpost words or phrases used by the professor ('The main point of this is . . .', etc.).

- Good lecturers tend to repeat important points – listen carefully for different examples or illustrations of a common theme.

- Try to think along with your professors by anticipating what's coming next.

- Note examples used by your professor and make sure that you understand their significance. If you don't understand the examples, ask the lecturer for advice. Professors like the feedback gained through students' questions.

- Ask yourself how this new information relates to what you already know.

- Get the name of at least one reference or assigned reading per lecture and consult it in the library or online.

Abbreviate, summarise and note key references

- Because professors tend to deliver their lectures quite rapidly, it helps to use abbreviations when taking notes (e.g. 'expt' for 'experiment' or 'FR' for 'French Revolution'). Be consistent with your abbreviation style and write a quick 'key' to explain the abbreviations at the top of the page – you may not remember what each one stands for later in the year.

- Usually, in the first few sentences, the professor will set the scene for the lecture presentation by providing both a summary of what was covered previously and an overview of what is to come. Pay close attention to these opening remarks.

- Write down any references that the professor mentions in class. You can check these references later in the library. If you can't manage to record the names accurately, ask the professor for these details immediately after the class or during her or his office hours.

What to do after your lectures: Reviewing your notes

If you're like most students, you put your lectures out of your mind as soon as they're over so that you can get on with your next activity. But research shows that going back over your lecture notes for 15–20 minutes later that day can boost your learning considerably (Putnam et al., 2016). Indeed, according to Miyatsu et al. (2018), the benefits of *reviewing* your notes are 'probably greater than the benefits of the act of taking notes' (p. 396). What exactly should you do?

Step 1:

Skim though your lecture notes for about 5 minutes. Remember that studying material regularly and briefly improves comprehension and memory retention. This is called 'spaced practice' or **'distributed practice'** (from Chapter 3).

Step 2:

Identify any points of confusion or uncertainty in your notes.

Step 3:

Turn these points into 2–3 specific questions that you can look up in your textbooks or ask your tutors and professors about during their office hours. An example for a psychology lecture might be 'What's the difference between negative reinforcement and punishment?'

Step 4:

Find out which specific chapters in your textbooks could help you to answer the questions that you've just written. Answering these questions should guide your studies.

Step 5:

Write 4–5 'topic sentences' to summarise the lecture. This exercise helps to build a bridge between the new material and what you already know about the topic in question.

Before concluding this chapter, let's return to a question that was raised earlier. Is it helpful to record lectures? See Box 4.4.

Box 4.4 Is it helpful to record lectures?

Is it a good idea to record lectures using your phone or computer? At first glance, it seems to make sense. After all, a recording gives you a simple and convenient method of capturing every word of the lecture. But, on closer inspection, recording lectures turns out to be a bad idea!

Firstly, it's ethically questionable if it's conducted without the explicit permission of the professor concerned and it may contravene university regulations. Also, you may have to obtain permission from your fellow students to record a lecture – especially if they ask questions or contribute to class discussion during it. More generally, professors are wary of having their classes recorded because of the uncertainty of where the recording will appear.

Apart from these issues, there are two psychological reasons why recording lectures is unwise. It induces passivity on the part of the listener. By contrast, the act of taking notes while listening to a lecture forces you to take an active role in thinking critically about its content.

In addition, you'll probably be very disappointed with the technical quality of any recording that you make during lectures. For example, you'll be amazed at how much background noise you can hear: coughs, seats shifting, talking among students – things that you never notice normally. This occurs because your mind, unlike computers, can filter out distractions.

For all these reasons, recording lectures is unethical and unwise – unless you have a good reason that precludes you from taking notes in the normal manner such as a visual impairment.

Now that I've covered learning from lectures, let's turn to the second topic of this chapter: how to get the most out of VLEs.

VLES AND DIGITAL LEARNING: THE IMPORTANCE OF INTERACTIVITY

As I explained earlier, VLEs are web-based systems that are accessible on a university's intranet but that hold external links. They enable students and professors to interact through digital learning activities. These systems facilitate learning in many ways: VLEs enable the storage and distribution of module content such as lecture notes and reading lists; they facilitate the collection and assessment of assignments; they allow the tracking of student engagement; they provide communication tools such as email and discussion boards. VLEs can be accessed easily and flexibly from laptops and mobile devices, both on and off-campus, 24 hours a day.

Why are VLEs important for digital learning? Three reasons spring to mind. There is evidence that academically successful students report greater use of digital technology to support, organise and manage their learning than do their less successful counterparts (Henderson et al., 2015). Psychologists have also shown that instruction using multimedia tools (which are available through VLEs) can improve your learning (Mayer, 2017). Finally, active engagement with technology-enhanced learning will help you to become an organised, efficient and enthusiastic 'e-learner', thereby increasing your employability significantly after graduation. As the New Media Consortium (NMC) Horizon Report concluded, 'the contemporary workforce calls for digitally-savvy employees who can seamlessly work with different media and new technologies as they emerge.' (Adams Becker et al., 2017, p. 7) In short, digital resources are extremely valuable when used at the right time and for the right purpose. For VLEs, that time is after you have attended a lecture, and the purpose is to consolidate what you have learned through self-evaluation and peer support.

Research on VLE usage among academics (Farrelly, Raftery, & Harding, 2018) and students (Raftery, 2018; Raftery & Risquez, 2018) highlights three important trends:

- In universities, VLEs tend to be used principally as 'content repositories' of lecture notes, module readings and links to websites and other digital resources.

- VLEs are employed routinely for assignment collection and management (with plagiarism detection software) and also for grading purposes.

- Within the VLE, methods of communication and inter-action, such as discussion boards, are currently used *less frequently* than tools for content management.

Taken together, these trends suggest that, although VLEs are effective in supporting student learning, their capacity for *inter-activity* is under-utilized at present. This is contrary to the design and usefulness of VLEs as a digital learning tool.

Building on the theme of interactivity, VLEs can facilitate a 'student-led' method of learning, whereby participants research information about a specific topic (see also Chapter 9), communicate their findings and raise discussion questions with each other. This type of learning contrasts sharply with the more traditional 'professor-led', didactic style of teaching apparent in lectures. VLEs provide opportunities for students to generate and share study questions with each other which, as we explained in Chapters 1 and 5, is the key to absorbing and retaining information. Clearly, using VLEs makes learning more interactive, enjoyable and long-lasting.

SOCIAL MEDIA

According to the University of Cambridge (2016), the term 'social media' (which can be either singular or plural) refers to a variety of online interactive communication tools that encourage partici-pation and exchanges between users. Lannin & Scott (2014) state that typical social media platforms include:

- Social networking sites such as Facebook

- Scientific networking sites like ResearchGate

- Publishing media such as Wordpress and Wikipedia

- Content-sharing sites like YouTube

- Discussion sites like Skype

- Microblogging sites such as Twitter

- Virtual worlds such as Second Life.

Many students use social media to discuss academic or professional matters in groups, pages, channels or threads created through platforms like Facebook, WhatsApp, YouTube, Vimeo and Twitter. Given that such social media facilitates campus-based communication and collaboration, can it be used to support learning activities in university? In addressing this question, Ahern, Feller, & Nagle (2016) investigated undergraduate students' use of Facebook Groups (i.e. student-led groups created by students for students) in studying Business Information Systems. These authors concluded that Facebook Groups provided 'an informal learning community' for students because they offered peer support and interaction concerning university-related issues (p. 47).

Given the prevalence of social media in university, here are some tips on getting the most out of them (McGraw Hill Education, 2015):

- Designate a module or study group hashtag that can be used on Twitter to share real-time questions, opinions and experiences relating to your coursework.

- Search for other groups of students in other parts of the world who are studying the same topic as you and ask them if they would like to share their questions, ideas and comments using Skype.

- If you're working on a group project, use Google Docs to store relevant documents.

- Use Facebook, Twitter and ResearchGate to follow authors of books or articles recommended for your module readings. ResearchGate is a social networking site that enables researchers to ask questions, share resources and find potential collaborators. These channels will help you to find out what relevant authors and researchers are working on at present and what new publications they have produced.

- Ask questions of experts during 'Ask Me Anything' (AMA) sessions on Twitter, blog websites or other apps.

ADVANTAGES OF VLES OVER SOCIAL MEDIA

If you already use social media such as Facebook and WhatsApp, you may wonder what the advantages are of engaging with VLEs: what can the latter platforms offer that most social media apps do not? (see also Box 4.5)

- **Administration and organisation:** VLEs typically provide a university calendar and specific details of all module timetables and assessments. This information will help you organise your study time effectively (see also Chapter 3).

- **Module content storage and distribution:** VLEs can store and distribute lecture notes, recommended readings and other module-relevant information.

- **Submission of assignments:** You can submit your assignments digitally through your VLE.

- **Checking your progress:** Most VLEs enable professors to generate self-assessment quizzes to test your under-standing of module content and associated readings. The 'formative feedback' (information on your strengths and weaknesses; see Chapter 10) that you receive from participating in these quizzes is invaluable.

- **Communication and collaboration**: VLEs facilitate communication and collaboration between students and tutors in an official space. Students can chat to tutors or other students within designated groups. This is parti-cularly helpful for distance learners or part-time students.

- **Inclusion**: Most VLEs have tools to enable professors to cater for students with special learning needs (e.g. visual or hearing impairments). They can also be used to gain access to online glossaries or translation software, which can help students whose first language is not English.

TIPS ON NETIQUETTE IN ACADEMIC COMMUNICATION: MINDING YOUR ONLINE BEHAVIOUR

The term 'netiquette' is the portmanteau for 'network etiquette' – the 'dos and don'ts' of online communication (Rutgers University, 2018). When you interact with your professors and fellow students, you are engaging in academic communication. It is your responsibility to read and adhere to your university's guidelines for such online behaviour. In addition, remember that the content, style and tone of your messages may create a psychological impression about your credibility, intelligence and dedication. Therefore, a good question to ask yourself before you hit the 'Reply' button is: 'Would I say this to someone face to face?' More generally, here are some guidelines for electronic communication in university (Cottrell & Morris, 2012; University of Waterloo, 2018).

Do:

- Read and adhere to your university's code of conduct. Universities can impose serious sanctions on students for intentional violation of this code such as engaging in online harassment or bullying.

- Use specific keywords in the subject heading or title of your messages. Remember that the title or heading of your message should reflect the content that will follow.

- Proofread your messages for logic, clarity and grammatical accuracy and try to make your points as concisely as possible.

- Assume that anyone to whom you send messages about a job, a reference or work experience will form impressions of you on the basis of how you present yourself in online communication. Make sure that such messages are always polite and professional.

- Check your privacy settings to make sure your posts are only shared with those with whom you want to communicate. Remember that anything that you share on social media, even in a private network, could be stored and circulated internationally.

- Be aware of copyright restrictions on material you share or use online. Always give credit to other people's written work, illustrations, photos or videos (see 'plagiarism' in Chapter 10).

Don't:

- Don't post any messages that you would not be happy to see on your university's homepage. Remember that, even in private groups, people can still take screenshots and share your information, photos and posts with others.

- Don't post messages written in haste or anger – you may regret them! It's all too easy to dash off a comment in the heat of the moment but then wish you could retract it later.

- Don't post inappropriate comments or images of yourself or send them as direct messages to other people in your group.

- Don't expect to get instant responses from your professors – especially when you contact them out of term time.

- Don't disagree with someone's point or argument through personal or hurtful comments. Instead, indicate the specific aspects of their statements or argument that you disagree with and support your point of view with appropriate evidence and in a respectful tone.

- Don't send messages typed in upper-case letters – it's the visual equivalent of shouting and is perceived as being aggressive and impolite.

GETTING THE MOST OUT OF VLES: PRACTICAL TIPS

As I explained in the introduction, you will discover the full benefits of using VLEs if you and your classmates actively participate in sharing and discussing module-relevant information. How can you get the most out of VLEs? See Box 4.5.

Box 4.5 Tips on the optimal use of VLEs

1   Find out how to log into your university's VLE and to how to use the app using a mobile device. Learn how to navigate the VLE, how to upload documents and images, how to set alerts, how to submit assignments and how to check feedback from the VLE's plagiarism detection software (Turnitin).

2   If lecture notes are available for upcoming classes, download and read them in advance. Download the files to a secure location on your desktop so that you can access them if the server or internet are down.

3   If you are able to create folders in your VLE, create a new one for every week of the academic year, which will help organise notes and research.

4   Invite other students to a group discussion either in person or via email. Check whether they would like to join the group first rather than adding them without their consent; otherwise, you could find people don't actively participate in the discussion, which lowers group morale.

5   If you are discussing a topic using group chat, try to type at a moderate pace so that everyone has a chance to reply to a comment. Too many replies from a single person can overwhelm the discussion and discourage others from participating.

6   If you find it difficult to participate in a group discussion by voicing an opinion or asking a question, try to participate by providing links to relevant articles or research. You are still adding to the group, albeit in a different way.

7   Use at least one message to summarise the main points or different sides of the topic when you feel the discussion is coming to a close.

8   Try to include a reason for agreeing or disagreeing with someone, or try to make a connection with something else ('Your point reminds me of an article I read that says that …').

9   Always provide evidence to support your opinions.

10 Don't take disagreement personally – focus on the evidence provided.

Remember: interactivity enriches your digital learning.

AUGMENTED AND VIRTUAL REALITY DIGITAL TOOLS

There are many other useful digital tools that offer a rich variety of learning experiences and are worth exploring. Among such environments are **augmented** and **virtual reality** tools. Typically, augmented reality is a form of digital technology that provides layers of computer-generated enhancements on top of existing reality in order to facilitate interaction with it. By contrast, virtual reality is an artificial, computer-generated simulation of a real-life environment or situation. It immerses users in a scenario or task, making them feel as though they are actually experiencing it. Augmented reality *supplements* your environment; virtual reality *replaces* it. In recent years, augmented and virtual reality environments have become increasingly popular in academic disciplines ranging from medicine (Nemani et al., 2018) to history (Harley et al., 2016) and languages (Chen, 2016; Lin & Yu-Ju, 2015).

A key feature of augmented reality environments, especially for students of architecture, engineering and medicine, is that they enable you to manipulate 3-D, multi-media information. Digitally-rendered objects can be turned and twisted so that you can view them from all angles. Interestingly, Peterson & Mlynarczyk (2016) compared anatomy students' examination performance on material that had been taught using either lecture and cadaveric dissection teaching tools alone or lecture and cadaveric dissection augmented with computerized 3-D teaching tools. Results showed that the addition of the 3-D tools improved students' retention of anatomical information. Research also shows that working with augmented reality enhances your ability to *evaluate* information as well as to recall it.

Virtual reality, as an alternative digital tool, offers a fully immersive environment – one that you are not currently occupying. It provides a safe environment that enables you to acquire skills and to experience situations that could be potentially dangerous in reality. One example of this is where medical students can practise incisions for surgery (Nemani et al., 2018).

Having explored the interactive opportunities offered by VLEs and other learning environments, I'd like to conclude this section of the chapter by addressing the question of how to evaluate online sources of information.

HOW TO CRITICALLY EVALUATE WEB SOURCES OF INFORMATION

A Google search gives you rapid access to a plethora of website information. But how can you determine their credibility and accuracy? Research requires you to *evaluate* information, not just to find it (see Chapter 7 for tips on 'critical thinking'). Here are some practical tips on evaluating website content (see Box 4.6).

Box 4.6 Critically evaluating website content: Practical tips

1 **Preview the website**: Read the title of the website and menu choices carefully. Are any headings relevant to your research question?

2 **Establish the scope and target audience**: Is the purpose of the website clearly defined: to inform you, to persuade you or to sell something to you? Who is the target audience? Does the written content accurately reflect the headline of the article? Is the website a personal one or attached to a reputable academic or research institution?

3 **Check the credibility of its source or authority**: Who created the information on the website? Is the name of the author clearly identified? If not, why would she or he remain anonymous? What are the credentials of the author? Is she or he an acknowledged and suitably qualified expert in the topic? Can you find any references in scholarly publications to this author's research or writing? Note that universities in certain countries have standardised domain names. UK universities typically end in '...ac.uk' and US universities end in '...edu'.

4 **Find out the online article's publication date**: Is the information on the website up-to-date (i.e. published in the last 2–3 years)? How frequently is the website updated? Are the links on the website up-to-date and working reliably?

5 **Verify the article's accuracy and that of any supporting evidence**: Has the content been peer-reviewed? Is it supported by relevant and verifiable evidence? Does it contain a list of references from peer-reviewed journals or other scholarly sources? Are these sources reliable and verifiable? Is the text well-written, grammatically correct and free of spelling errors? Are additional references or scholarly sources of evidence provided?

6 **Look for objectivity of coverage**: Does the author present objective arguments, or is the content based on personal opinion only or slanted in any way? Does the website present only one theoretical perspective on the issue or are multiple perspectives available to you? How similar is the author's view or ideas to those of other researchers in the field with whom you are familiar? Is the website part of an organisation with a particular political agenda? Does the website contain advertising or promote certain products or ideas uncritically?

SUMMARY

The formal lecture is the most popular teaching method in university. Normally, it involves a professor delivering a presentation on a specific topic for about 50 minutes, typically supported by multimedia. Unfortunately, it can be difficult to take useful lecture notes because professors tend to speak much faster than you can write. The good news, however, is that lecture notes are normally available through your university's VLE, a web-based learning management system that enables professors and students to interact using a variety of digital tools. The purpose of this chapter, therefore, was to give you some practical tips on learning from lectures and from VLEs.

In the introduction, I explained that good note-taking requires active listening – *thinking along with* your professors to such an extent that you can 'see' where the lecture is going. This interactive approach encourages you to develop a deep understanding of lecture content because you're trying to link new material with what you already know. Interestingly, interactivity (asking questions and sharing ideas with fellow students) applies as much to learning from VLEs as it does to learning from lectures.

Following a discussion of the cognitive challenge of learning from lectures, which involves learning to think and write simultaneously, I explored common barriers to learning from lectures and gave you practical strategies to overcome them. Among these strategies were:

1 Developing a pre-lecture routine

2 Learning how to take lecture notes selectively

3 Organising the lecture in your mind

4 Paying special attention to professors' signpost words

5 Learning to use abbreviations

6 Reviewing your lecture notes after class.

In the next section of the chapter, I highlighted the importance of VLEs and explored some of their advantages over informal social media. Then, I considered netiquette in communication and gave you some 'dos and don'ts' when engaging in online behaviour with fellow students and professors.

The next part of the chapter was devoted to improving your learning from VLEs. A key theme of this section was that you need to go beyond using VLEs for logistical purposes (e.g. downloading lecture notes) and, instead, embrace their potential for *interactivity* by communicating and collaborating as often as possible with other students and your professors on module-related learning tasks.

In the final section of the chapter, I gave you a practical checklist of questions to use in order to critically evaluate online sources of information such as websites. This checklist included advice on previewing the website:

- Establishing its scope and target audience

- Checking the credibility of its source or authority

- Finding out the publication date of its information

- Verifying its accuracy and that of any supporting evidence

- Looking for objectivity of coverage.

Answer to exercise in Box 4.3 (p. 56)
The heading is 'A Guide to Washing Clothes'.

CURIOUSLY ENOUGH, ONE CANNOT READ A BOOK: ONE CAN ONLY RE-READ IT. A GOOD READER, A MAJOR READER, AN ACTIVE AND CREATIVE READER IS A RE-READER.

Vladimir Nabokov (1980)

Chapter 5

Tackling Textbooks
Improving Your Reading and Summarising Skills

INTRODUCTION

One of the most striking features of university education is the sheer extent of background reading you're expected to undertake for your degree. If you're studying for a multiple-choice exam (MCQ), preparing a lab report or writing a final-year research project, you'll have to read lots of textbooks, monographs and papers in academic journals. In addition to this quantitative challenge is a qualitative one – the fact that you're expected to *think for yourself* or form evidence-based conclusions about what you have read. Put simply, you not only have to read more in university than in school but you also to read *differently* (as hinted at by Nabokov in the quote above). But has anyone ever taught you how to extract maximum information from what you read? If not, then you may benefit from some practical advice on this skill. The purpose of this chapter is to show you how to read more deeply, systematically and effectively than at present.

This chapter is organised as follows:
....

> ➤ I'll outline a brief explanation of what reading involves.
> ➤ I'll provide some practical advice on how to cope with daunting course syllabi and their associated reading lists.

➤ Following an analysis of some reading strategies used by experts, I'll show you how to use a technique called the 'PQRR' method. This technique trains you to process written material deeply and efficiently.

➤ By contrast, I'll explain why underlining, highlighting, transcription and photocopying are largely a waste of time.

➤ I'll explain how to improve your summarising skills.

➤ I'll show you how to judge a book by its cover – or at least assess the quality of your textbooks.

READING

Cognitive processes such as memory are brain-based skills that we use to make sense of the world. Many such processes contribute to the skill of reading, which is typically defined as the processing of textual information in order to decode the meaning of each word, phrase and sentence (Rayner et al., 2016). Like all cognitive skills, reading improves with practice. Indeed, as a result of thousands of hours of practice from early childhood, most adults' reading is so fast, fluent and effortless (200–400 words per minute) that we notice it only when it *fails* in some way. For example, when we come across an unfamiliar technical term such as 'homoscedasticity', an uncommon adjective such as 'prolix' or an apparently unintelligible sentence (see sentence 3 of Box 5.1), our word recognition skills come to a sudden halt.

Box 5.1 What on earth does this mean?

Here is an extract from an article published in *The Irish Times* (Crawley, 2015). Can you understand the third sentence?

'The relationship between theatre and academia is somewhere between an intimate appreciation and an endearingly awkward encounter. One is attractive and mysterious, full of meanings, rich histories and teasing signals. The other is a fervent admirer who would reveal to it (and anyone interested) its inner secrets, wider significance and, occasionally, mnemonic imperatives towards self-fragilising interaction within the matrixial border space' (p. 13).

When our ability to make sense of words and sentences breaks down, we realise that reading is more complex than it seems. For example, as I'll show you shortly, it involves *drawing inferences* implicitly from the text. To discover this for yourself, try the exercise in Box 5.2.

Box 5.2 Reading involves drawing inferences

When we read, we automatically draw inferences from the text. For example, consider the following two sentences. Do they make sense as they are presented or do you have to draw on your background knowledge to interpret them?

Example 1   When the attacker went down in the box, the referee blew the whistle and pointed to the spot.

Example 2   When the policewoman held up her hand, the man stopped and rolled down his window.

Example 3   Mary heard the ice cream van coming down the road. She ran into her house to get some money.

Most readers conclude that the first sentence refers to a penalty awarded during a football or a hockey match. But notice that the word 'penalty' isn't mentioned in the sentence – it's something that you *inferred* from the text using your background knowledge of sport. Similarly, in order to interpret the second sentence, you probably inferred that the man was driving a car and that police officers have the power to request drivers to stop. Finally, in the third example, you may have concluded that Mary went into her house to get some money to buy ice cream. Notice that this was *never actually stated* in the text – you implicitly supplied the missing details using your database of background knowledge. Overall, these examples show you that reading is an active, constructive process which requires the unconscious use of background knowledge to build up an understanding of the writer's intended message.

Skilled reading is a remarkable cognitive feat. To illustrate, based on your ability to read this book, you can probably identify up to 30,000 words in a fraction of a second. This is true even when these words are handwritten or printed in a variety of different font sizes and styles (Rayner et al., 2012). Effective reading requires at least three types of mental processing activities.

1 As Box 5.2 shows, you need to be able to use relevant background knowledge to fill in any gaps in what you read.

2 Your word recognition skills must be effortless or else your reading will be slow and cumbersome.

3 You have to check regularly that you *understand* what you're reading. Without such comprehension monitoring (see Chapter 1), little or no learning will occur.

Overall, therefore, reading is not a passive process. Instead, it's an active and predictive activity in which the reader interrogates the text in search of meaning. Paradoxically, skilled readers don't just absorb information from a passage of text, they *add background knowledge* to it in order to make sense of it. That's why reading is called a **constructive activity**: you build an understanding of the meaning of the text.

To illustrate the constructive nature of your reading, you should have no difficulty in understanding the following sentence even though more than a third of the letters are missing.

Thx pxssxblx mexnxxg ox a sxxtenxe ix quxte exsy tx extxblxsh whxn yxur mxnd fillx ix thx gapx.

If you can't decipher this piece of text, please turn to the summary at the end of the chapter for the answer. If you've worked out what the sentence means, you've discovered that reading involves the imaginative 'building up' of meaning. Ironically, it is this constructive process, or the automatic habit of filling in the blanks in what you read, which explains why it can be difficult for us to spot typing errors when we proofread our own writing. For example, have you ever missed a duplicated word in an essay that you wrote despite reading over it several times?

To be a good reader, you need at least four skills.

1 You must be able to move your eyes swiftly across the page to 'encode' or 'take in' the text visually (see Chapter 8 for an explanation of encoding).

2   In order to understand the material, you need rapid access to a large vocabulary of word meanings (your mental lexicon).

3   Your working memory (the system that controls your concentration) must be efficient. For example, if you're reading a long sentence, you must be able to put the initial words of the sentence 'on hold' while you process the meaning of the last few words.

4   You have to be good at drawing inferences from the text – filling in details that were omitted but implied – using your background knowledge.

Now that you understand the key mental activities involved in reading, I'd like to raise another question. What strategies do you think *expert* readers use when tackling a paper in their specialist field? To answer this question, Wyatt et al. (1993) analysed the behaviour of a sample of active social scientists as they read self-selected professional articles related to their specialist fields. These professors were then requested to think aloud as they read the selected articles. Their comments were audio recorded and their eye-movements were measured using an eye-tracker. Results showed that the expert readers:

- Looked for information relevant to their own research questions
- Summarised key points frequently
- Tried to anticipate information in the text
- Searched the text – looking forwards and backwards for specific information
- Re-read sentences that were unclear
- Evaluated new information from the text in the light of what they already knew
- Checked their progress as they read through the article.

What's interesting about these findings is that they're remarkably similar to those describing what successful students do when they read textbooks (see Box 1.2) – searching, reviewing and checking frequently. Therefore, it seems that expert readers – whether eminent professors or successful students – differ from relative novices by using a host of active learning techniques such as interrogating the text in search of answers to questions and checking understanding regularly. Fortunately, you can implement precisely the same approach using the PQRR reading technique, which I'll explain shortly. Before doing so, I'll address the problem of how to cope with intimidating course syllabi and lengthy reading lists.

HELP! COPING WITH COURSE SYLLABI AND READING LISTS

Ideally, a course syllabus is a document that accurately and explicitly outlines the nature, scope and requirements of a module. For example, it should include the module title and code; the names and contact details of the professors involved; module objectives or goals; a list of topics to be covered along with a specific lecture schedule; assessment details (i.e. how students will be examined); and a reading list. If any of these details are unclear, ask the professor concerned. Of these details, students tend to struggle most with the reading list.

A reading list is a compilation of references which a professor deems to be either essential or relevant to her or his course or module. Typically, reading lists provide background information on a subject area as well as specific resources for course assignments. Unfortunately, all too often, reading lists are lengthy and forbidding – thereby demoralising, rather than inspiring, students. How can you manage your reading lists effectively? Box 5.3 provides some practical tips for this task.

Box 5.3 Managing your reading lists

1　Print several copies of the list so that you can store them with your lecture notes and on your study desk.

2　You don't have to read every item on the list. Distinguish between essential and recommended readings. If this information is not stated explicitly, ask your professor for help.

3 For essential readings, find out which ones are available to borrow from the library or which can be read electronically via the library e-books.

4 Distinguish between primary and secondary sources. The former include original works whereas the latter contain commentaries on, or analysis of, this material.

5 If possible, talk to students who have taken this course before and ask them for tips on which readings were most useful to them.

When you have decided which books you wish to tackle, the next step is to learn to read them thoroughly. This brings us to an expert reading strategy called the PQRR technique.

BECOMING AN EXPERT READER: THE PQRR TECHNIQUE

One of the great pioneers of reading strategies was an educational psychologist named Francis Robinson of Ohio State University. He devised the technique on which the PQRR strategy is based (Robinson, 1961). This acronym represents four key steps in efficient reading: previewing, questioning, reading and reviewing. To illustrate these skills in action, imagine that you wish to read a specific chapter from a textbook on your course.

Preview – 'P'

To begin with, preview or skim the chapter for 2–3 minutes before you read it in detail. Not previewing a chapter is like walking into a darkened room without turning on the light – you won't know where you're going (Deem, 1993). As you skim through the pages, pay attention to the flow of ideas and the titles of the paragraphs and glance over any summaries that might be provided. Previewing what you read is helpful in at least three ways.

1 It gives you a taste of what's to come – just like watching a film trailer.

2 It activates your background knowledge or expectations about the topic.

3 It helps to establish hooks or cues which facilitate later retrieval (see also Chapter 8).

Practical tips on previewing

- Look at the headings of the sections and paragraphs of the chapter in order to 'get a feel' for the way in which it is organised.

- Glance at the name of any pictures, charts, diagrams, graphs and tables.

- Look for signpost words which suggest important conclusions ('To summarise' or 'Overall').

- Skim through any summaries which may be available at the end of the chapter.

Question – 'Q'

Asking questions is the key to active learning for three main reasons.

1 It helps you to challenge assumptions, expose contradictions and to close the gap between what you currently know and what you'd like to know.

2 It hijacks your thoughts momentarily (Hoffield, 2017). To illustrate, what colour is the door to your house or apartment? Once you have been asked that question, you'll find it hard to think about anything else until you find the answer! Questions switch on your concentration system, even for a moment.

3 It activates your brain. For example, a neuroimaging study by Gruber, Gelman, & Ranganath (2014) found that a high state of curiosity triggers brain circuits involved in motivation and memory.

For these three reasons, it's important to write down 2–3 specific questions before you open a book chapter. Sample questions for different subjects are provided in Box 5.4.

Your study questions can come from a wide variety of sources. For example, they could spring from personal experience: 'How common is loneliness among first year university students?' They could come from general interest:'Do social media influencers affect our buying behaviour?' They could be prompted by a remark made by one of your professors: 'Sir Arthur Conan Doyle wrote the first Victorian detective novel'. If you're more practically-minded, you could get your question from a previous year's examination paper: 'How are molecular techniques used in the attempt to diagnose diseases?'

Practical tips on questioning

- What is the main theme, idea or learning point in this chapter?

- How does this theme relate to what I already know?

- What evidence, arguments or examples are cited by the author(s) to support what they say? (see also Chapter 7).

Box 5.4 Sample study questions

Subject	Topic	Question
Veterinary medicine	Animal science	What factors affect growth rate in animals?
Law	Constitutional law	How does the constitution regulate the government's entry into, and departure from, office?
Science	Geology	How may silicate minerals can be classified according to their atomic structure?
Medicine	Histology	What are the characteristic features of a monosynaptic reflex arc?
Statistics	Correlation	What is a correlation coefficient and how is it calculated?

Subject	Topic	Question
Social Science	Social policy	What factors led to the development of a Welfare State in Britain after World War II?
Physiotherapy or radiography	Biochemistry	Why are some amino acids referred to as non-essential?
Engineering	Manufacturing technology	What is re-crystallisation?
Agricultural science	Chemistry	Why does sodium form an anion but magnesium does not?
Italian	Grammar	What are the basic rules for the use of definite and indefinite articles in Italian?
History	Modern Irish	What events led to the Irish revolution (1918–23)?
Marketing	Advertising	What constitutes 'good' advertising?
Accountancy	Fixed assets	What are 'fixed assets' and how can we value them?
Science	Biology	How does a cell synthesise aprotein molecule from an mRNA template?

Read – 'R'

Read the chapter carefully with your study questions in mind. This questioning style of reading is what experts use to enable them to *think* while they read. As you make your way through the chapter, make brief notes to help you answer your study questions. Material is relevant if it provides answers to your specific study questions and irrelevant if it fails to do so.

Practical tips on reading

- Always read with a pen and paper beside you. Remember that you're *looking for answers* to 2–3 specific questions.

- Write down any information that seems to provide answers to any of your study questions.

- Try to locate a 'topic sentence' that summarises what the author believes to be the most important point in a paragraph or chapter.

- Slow down if you come to a difficult passage. If you don't understand something, you should go back ('I can't understand this point: I'd better go back a few paragraphs') or forwards ('I'll skip ahead to see if this point is clarified in a later section') until the point makes sense to you.

- Note any difficult technical terms so that you can look them up later.

Review – 'R'

The final stage of active reading consists of checking your understanding of the material by *reviewing* what you have learned. One way of doing this is by examining the notes on your summary sheet and checking the degree to which they answer your initial study questions. Alternatively, if you participate in a regular study group with some classmates, you could explain what you learned from the chapter and encourage your listeners to ask you questions about this material. When you have finished reviewing what you have learned, you should then consult another textbook with the same set of study questions in mind. Comparing answers from different textbooks to the same study questions encourages critical thinking (see also Chapter 7).

Practical tips on reviewing

- Pause from time to time to ask yourself what you have learned from the chapter.

- Glance over your summary sheets that hold the answers to your study questions before you put away your books.

Box 5.5 Using the PQRR technique

Pick a chapter from a textbook that you wish to study. Then, using the PQRR approach, fill in the details below.

Step 1: Preview the chapter

Skim through the pages of this chapter for 3–5 minutes using the practical tips outlined earlier on previewing skills. Then see if you can answer the following questions:

- What topic does this chapter cover? Can you turn this topic into precise questions? For example, if the topic were inflation, some questions might be: What is inflation? How can we measure it? Why is it important?

- What ideas (if any!) come to mind when you think about this topic? You might wonder about the names of theorists, for example.

Step 2: Formulate 2–3 specific questions

What are your specific study questions for this chapter?

Step 3: Read with your questions in mind

Read through the text with your 2–3 study questions in mind. Pause from time to time to check your progress by asking yourself 'What have I learned so far?' Summarise relevant information such as definitions or theories on a sheet of paper beside each of your questions but ignore all other details.

Step 4: Review your summary sheet

When you have finished reading the chapter, ask yourself:

- What did I learn?

- How does it relate to what I already know?

Now that you have discovered the value of the PQRR reading technique, let's explore some ineffective (e.g. underlining) and effective (e.g. summarising) ways of learning from textbooks.

LEARNING FROM TEXTBOOKS

Now that you have discovered the value of the PQRR reading technique, let's explore some intuitively appealing yet ineffective strategies of learning from textbooks. Three such strategies are: underlining selected passages of the text in pen or pencil or highlighting them with a fluorescent marker – a strategy called 'marking'; transcribing textbook material verbatim; and photocopying as much of the book as possible. Why are these strategies ineffective?

Why underlining, highlighting, transcribing and photocopying are inefficient

To begin with, marking the text by underlining or highlighting it has many weaknesses. Firstly, students often mark irrelevant information or else engage in 'mindless marking' of too much text (Miyatsu et al., 2018). Secondly, when students re-read a marked textbook, they are vulnerable to 'habituation' effects where people stop noticing something that was initially distinctive (in this case, the marked text) the more they encounter it. Thirdly, and perhaps most seriously, marking a book does not produce any notes for you. When you close your book, the marked text is no longer visible.

What about transcription as a learning strategy? The problem here is similar to that of trying to take down every word that a professor utters in class: the material goes straight into your notes, without any elaboration or re-organisation on your part.

The third strategy involves photocopying everything in sight. In this case, students make the false assumption that possession is equivalent to comprehension (a myth called the 'seduction of reproduction') – if you have a photocopy of an article, then you'll get around to understanding it someday. Of course, this theory is wrong. When Francis Bacon said that knowledge was power, he was *not* referring to stacks of unread photocopies! Unless you can summarise or paraphrase accurately what is in a photocopied document, you may as well not have it at all.

Overall, the main weakness of the three preceding strategies is that they don't enable you to produce a *summary* of the material you've read. Accordingly, these techniques are mindless because they neither reduce the amount of material to be processed nor do they help you to distinguish between relevant and irrelevant information in the book. By contrast, the act of *summarising* a passage of text *in your own words* helps you develop a personal understanding of it (see also Chapter 8). Therefore, the best way to approach a textbook is to summarise material in selected chapters that is most relevant to the questions that you're trying to answer. All other strategies are largely a waste of time.

THE COGNITIVE BENEFITS OF SUMMARISING AND WHY YOU HAVE TO WRITE YOUR OWN SUMMARIES

Making a concise summary of something will help you in at least four ways:

1   It reduces the amount of material that you have to learn.

2   It forces you to *think critically* about what you are reading because you have to distinguish between information that answers your study questions (relevant material) and that which doesn't (irrelevant material).

3   Summarising helps you to link new material to what you already know – a process called elaborative rehearsal (see also Chapter 8).

4   Summaries provide template answers to possible exam questions.

But why should you make a summary of an article or a book if that work has already been done by the author(s)? After all, most journal papers contain an abstract that provides a succinct summary of the purpose, method, results and conclusions of the article. Similarly, most textbooks provide chapter summaries. The answer is deceptively simple. Abstracts and chapter summaries are the *authors'* synopses of their work – not *your* summary of what's relevant to *your* specific questions. That's why your summary will invariably differ from their ones. It's designed to answer your personal study questions.

CAN YOU JUDGE A BOOK BY ITS COVER . . . OR OTHER FEATURES?

Can you judge the quality of a book by its cover? More precisely, how does the design of an academic book affect its readability?

Before I answer this latter question, here's a little puzzle for you. Think of a specific textbook on your course. Can you name the sections of this book that appear before the beginning of Chapter 1? If you have trouble remembering sections like the 'Preface', 'Foreword', 'Introduction' and 'Table of Contents', then you're not paying enough attention to the *structure* of your books. The point is that the design of an academic textbook is not accidental. Each section, ranging from the title page to the index, plays a specific role in helping you to locate and understand its content. With this idea in mind, here are some practical tips on evaluating textbooks (based on Marshall & Rowland, 2014).

Title and subtitle

Note the key words used (e.g. 'motor cognition') and look for any information revealed by subtitles (e.g. 'an embodiment approach'). This subtitle will reveal any theoretical perspectives favoured by the author.

Cover or dust jacket

Skim through any information about the author and the book on the back cover or dust jacket. This information may indicate any novel features of this book (e.g. its role in filling a gap in the literature or in providing a critical review of the field).

Biographical details of author(s)

Scan any biographical information on the author(s) of the book. What research institution are they affiliated to and what are their specialist research expertise?

Publication details

When was the book published, who published it and what edition does it represent (e.g. second, fifth)? The more recently published the book, the more likely it is to contain up-to-date research findings.

Table of Contents
Flicking through the table of contents, you can quickly establish which of the chapters are most relevant to your specific questions.

Preface, Foreword and Introduction
The preface, foreword and introduction usually provide answers to such questions as: *Why was this book written? How does it build on previous books in the field? What makes it different from its predecessors? What's new or different about the approach adopted by the author?*

Chapter structure
As with the title of the book, the heading of each chapter indicates the topic that will receive coverage. And shown in Box 1.3 on p. 8, a good way to increase your interest in it is simply to turn all titles into questions (e.g. 'Quadratic equations' becomes 'What are quadratic equations?'). In addition, the structure of the chapters is important. For example, is a summary provided at the end of each chapter? If so, you should read it before working your way through the chapter.

Glossary
If the book has a glossary at the end, skim through it in advance to see if you can recognise any of the terms it contains.

Bibliography and references
Is there a bibliography or list of references at the end of the book? If not, and if you cannot find any footnotes or end-notes either, then you should be sceptical of the academic credibility of the book. Without references, how can you validate the author's opinions? If you know some of the names of key researchers in this field, try to find out if these people are listed among the references.

Subject and author index
The index of a book will help you to check whether or not key names and concepts are referred to in the main body of the book. A short index may suggest that the book is not very comprehensive in scope.

SUMMARY

At university, you are expected to engage in a type of reading that is both quantitatively and qualitatively different from what you've done previously. But *how* can you extract maximum information from what you read? The purpose of this chapter was to show you how to read more deeply, systematically and effectively than at present.

- I began with a brief explanation of what reading involves.

- I provided some practical advice on how to cope with daunting course syllabi and their associated reading lists.

- Following analysis of some reading strategies used by experts, I showed you how to use a technique called the 'PQRR' technique to process written material deeply and efficiently.

- I explained why underlining, highlighting, transcription and photocopying are largely a waste of time.

- I gave you some practical tips on how to improve your summarising skills.

- Finally, I showed you how to judge a book by its cover – or at least assess the quality of your textbooks.

Answer to sentence on p. 76
'The possible meaning of a sentence is quite easy to establish when your mind fills in the gaps.'

DON'T FOCUS ON THE GUY NEXT TO YOU. HE MIGHT BE VERY QUICK OFF THE BLOCKS, WHICH CAN MAKE YOU LOSE CONCENTRATION. STAY FOCUSED ON WHAT YOU'RE GOING TO DO AND RUN YOUR OWN RACE ALL THE TIME.

Usain Bolt, Olympic gold medal-winner
Staph (2011)

Chapter 6

How to Focus Effectively
Improving Your Concentration Skills

INTRODUCTION

We are constantly bombarded by information. Every waking moment of the day, we face decisions about what to prioritise and what to ignore. To complicate matters, the information clamouring for our attention includes not only events that happen in the world around us but also experiences that spring from the private well of our own thoughts and feelings. In an effort to avoid **cognitive overload**, our minds can consciously pay attention to only a tiny fraction of the rich kaleidoscope of information available to us at any given time. Concentration, or the ability to focus on the task at hand while ignoring distractions, is vital for successful performance in every area of life, from the classroom to the sports field. In the latter case, Usain Bolt advises us to focus on *our own behaviour* when competing against others: run your own race.

Unfortunately, the brain process that controls our concentration – a system called **working memory** – is very limited in capacity. Working memory controls our ability to hold information in our minds for short periods of time while we work on it. Think of the numbers 26 and 39 – now subtract the smaller number from the larger. Your brain uses its working memory to do this. The major weakness of working memory, however, is that it's easily overloaded. For example, try *multiplying* 39 by 26 in your head. It's difficult, isn't it? Mental multiplication requires many more intermediate steps than does subtraction – and regrettably, these steps 'leak' quickly from your working memory.

The practical implication of having a fragile working memory is that it leads to chronic distractibility. For example, have you ever discovered that you've passively read the same sentence in a book over and over again without any comprehension because your mind was miles away? Do you sometimes find yourself thinking of something else during a lecture? Or have you ever gone from one room to another in search of something only to realise that you have forgotten what you were looking for? If you say 'yes' to any of these questions, then you have first-hand experience of everyday lapses in concentration.

But what exactly is concentration? Why do we lose it so easily? Perhaps, most importantly, what practical strategies could help you to focus more effectively? The purpose of this chapter is to provide some answers to these and other relevant questions.

This chapter is organised as follows:
....

> ➤ I'll explain what concentration is and how it works.
> ➤ I'll explore what distractions are, where they come from and how to overcome them.
> ➤ I'll show you how to improve your focusing skills when studying.

....

WHAT IS CONCENTRATION AND HOW DOES IT WORK? EXPLORING YOUR MENTAL SPOTLIGHT

Concentration is the ability to focus on what is most important in any situation while ignoring distractions. This could take the form of listening actively to your professor during a lecture while there is noise and movement around you in the theatre or classroom. What's the best way to understand concentration?

For many psychologists, concentration resembles the head-mounted torch that miners, divers and potholers wear when exploring dark environments. Wherever these adventurers shine their spotlights, their target is illuminated and they can pay attention to it. Building on this idea, the beam of your mental spotlight can be either broad or narrow. A broad attentional focus gives you a quick overview of a situation. To illustrate, when you enter a lecture theatre, you have a general awareness of movement and noise as your classmates look for seats and chat to each other while taking out their notes. However, your attentional focus will probably become narrower when the professor begins to speak. If you become completely absorbed in what she or he is saying because of your interest in the topic, your mind is truly focused. In such rare moments, there's no difference between what you're thinking about and what you're *doing*. Interestingly, it is this elusive state of mind which characterises 'flow' experiences – those rare moments where total absorption in the task at hand leads to peak performance in sport, music and other fields (Swann et al., 2017).

Interestingly, there's one major difference between your mental spotlight and a mechanical torch. Your spotlight can shine *inwards* as well as outwards. To illustrate, imagine that, during a lecture, your mind begins to wander as you think about a social event that you're planning for the weekend. In this situation, you've distracted yourself by allowing a daydream to capture your attention. This brings us to an important lesson: you can never *'lose'* your concentration because your mental spotlight must be shining *somewhere*, But you *can* divert it to something that's irrelevant to the task at hand – like planning your weekend when you should be listening to your professor. That's what Usain Bolt meant when he warned of how easy it is to 'lose your concentration'. Remember – you're in control of where you shine your mental spotlight. That's why it's so important to have a specific study question in mind before you open your textbook. Instead of thinking, 'It would be good to study tonight if I have time,' it's much better to say, 'Between 7 and 8 pm tonight, I'm going to use my chemistry book to look up why sodium forms an anion whereas magnesium does not.'

In general, the ability to focus effectively requires three steps.

1 You have to *decide* to concentrate – it won't happen accidentally. Remember from Chapter 1 that studying involves *deliberate* learning. It's not like switching aimlessly from one television channel to another until you find something interesting to watch. Instead, studying requires a decision to invest mental effort in what you're doing.

2　You must have a *target* in mind – namely, a specific study question. However, given the brevity of your attention span, you need to write this question down or you won't remember it.

3　Remind yourself to *re-focus regularly* on the task at hand: otherwise you may end up being distracted.

DISTRACTIONS

The term 'distraction' means anything that diverts our mental spotlight from its intended target (e.g. a specific thought or action), thereby hampering our ability to focus on the job at hand. Interestingly, according to Fabritius and Hagemann your brain is a 'distraction-detection device' (p. 86, 2017) because it's driven to notice anything new or different in the world around you. That's why it's very difficult to ignore email alerts that pop up from time to time on your laptop screen while you're working (but see Box 6.1).

Although distractions come in all shapes and sizes, they can be divided into two main categories based on where they come from: external (from the outside world) and internal (from your own thoughts and feelings) (Moran, 1996).

External distractions

External distractions are things in the environment (e.g. people, events and situations) that divert your concentration from the job at hand. A typical distraction in this category is the ubiquitous habit of constantly checking digital devices such as your phone and laptop while studying.

Box 6.1　Overcoming digital distractions

How often do you check your social media platforms while attempting to study? If you're like most students, you'll probably find it difficult to resist the allure of digital distractions. How can you overcome this problem? Here are some practical tips on how to plan your digital detox.

1　Take planned 'tech check' breaks – but set a timer

Plan a short 'tech check' break after about 40 minutes of study to check your digital device (allow yourself 3 minutes only – use a timer). If you get a message about something important, make a note of it and then get ready to resume your study session.

2   Turn off your notifications

To avoid being distracted by unwanted 'beeps' and 'pings' from your phone, turn off your notifications while studying.

3   Out of sight, out of mind

Make it hard to check your phone by putting it out of sight or out of hearing while you study.

4   Take a break from social media

If you're constantly fighting an urge to use social media sites while you study, you're at risk of developing an addiction to technology – the habit of doing something that you like in the short-term that challenges your well-being in the long-term (Alter, 2017). To counteract this problem, take a break from at least one social media site for a week or two.

5   Give FOMO a rest

Don't let FOMO (fear of missing out) control your use of digital media late at night. It could impair your sleep. Winding down is important for a good night's rest.

6   Your attention is valuable: so how do you want to spend it?

Your attention is a valuable resource that app companies want: but how do you want to invest your mental effort? In the long run, it's best invested in your studies.

Internal distractions

Internal distractions are any thoughts, feelings or bodily sensations such as tiredness that prevent you from focusing on the job at hand. Typical distractions in this category are personal problems and a tendency to think too far ahead: *What if I don't do well in my exams?*

Why is it so difficult to block such distracting thoughts? The answer lies in Box 6.2.

Box 6.2 Don't think of a white bear! Dealing with distracting thoughts

The term 'mental control' refers to our ability to think what we want to think or to do what we intend to do. Although we're normally good at performing this skill, sometimes it fails. One person who noticed this was the Russian writer Dostoevsky, who observed that, occasionally, it can be very difficult not to think about something that you are asked to ignore. 'Try to pose for yourself this task: not to think of a polar bear, and you will see that the cursed thing will come to mind every minute' (cited in Winerman, 2011, p. 44). Intrigued by this paradox of thought suppression, Wegner (1994) demonstrated experimentally that people who had been explicitly instructed to *avoid* thinking of a white bear couldn't do so. Furthermore, he showed that when people are tired or anxious, they become *increasingly* aware of the thought that they are trying to suppress. So, if you try to fall asleep quickly because you're worried about missing a flight early the following morning, you may become even more alert!

In trying to explain this paradox, Wegner's (1994) theory of 'ironic processes' suggests that when we try *not* to think of something, the conscious part of our mind manages to avoid the unwanted thought. Unfortunately, the unconscious part 'checks in' regularly to make sure that the forbidden thought is locked away – thereby, ironically, making it more accessible to consciousness.

How can we suppress distracting thoughts and exert mental control successfully? Three strategies seem to work.

1   Immerse yourself in the present moment: focusing on the task at hand 'hijacks' your thoughts and reduces the likelihood of being distracted.

2   Postpone the distracting thought: setting aside a specific time every day to note your worries may prevent you from ruminating about them constantly (e.g. 15 mins in the evening).

3   Try mindfulness meditation: learning to accept your thoughts and feelings (i.e. *noticing* them rather than judging or commenting on them) improves your mental control (see also Box 6.3).

OVERCOMING DISTRACTIONS

Having explained what distractions are and where they come from, here are some practical suggestions for overcoming them.

- Try to clear your head of any worries before you begin to study.

- Find a quiet place to study without being disturbed.

- Keep your desk as a work place, not a storage place.

- Just start studying – don't wait to be in the right mood.

- Set a realistic goal for every study session, such as answering one question in 40–50 minutes.

- Always set a starting time and a finishing time for your study sessions.

- Make a daily list of study tasks and check your progress every night.

- Take regular exercise to clear your mind, such as a walk in the evening (see also Chapter 3).

- Give yourself visible reminders written on post-it notes to re-focus.

In the next section of this chapter, I'll give you some practical tips on improving your focusing skills.

PRACTICAL CONCENTRATION TECHNIQUES

Psychologists have developed a number of practical techniques that help to improve concentration skills. Many of these concentration techniques are based on methods used by leading athletes to achieve an optimal focus for their performance, as displayed in Figure 1 (Moran & Toner, 2017). Here are some of these techniques adapted for use in study situations.

Establish a study routine

Have you ever noticed that expert performers such as athletes and musicians tend to follow a consistent preparatory routine before they perform key skills? For example, top tennis players like to bounce the ball a certain number of times before serving and rugby kickers like to go through a systematic series of steps before striking the ball. These preferred action sequences are called '**pre-performance routines**' (Moran & Toner, 2017) and are widely used to improve concentration skills. The logic here is that, by immersing themselves in each step of their routine, performers stay focused on the present moment and are able to block out distractions. Do you have a consistent pre-study routine? If not, here are some questions to help you to develop one (see also Chapter 2).

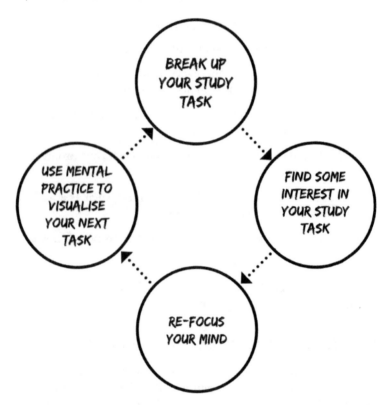

Figure 6.1: Study routine

- What is your ideal concentration time during the day? Morning, afternoon or evening?
- Do you have a quiet place in which to study?
- Have you developed the habit of studying in this place at the same time every day?
- Do you have 2–3 specific study questions?
- Have you written these questions down on a blank sheet of paper?
- Do you have the textbooks or notes that you need to answer these questions?
- Have you planned a reward for yourself after you've answered your study questions?

Break up your study task: Use means-end analysis

Many academic assignments seem difficult because of the way in which they're presented to us. For example, being asked to write an essay on a new topic or to review a paper is a daunting challenge. But if you break this challenge down into a series of sub-problems that can be solved separately, the assignment becomes much more manageable and enjoyable. A good way to tackle your essay or paper assignment is by writing a background paragraph or a summary of three key studies on the topic in question (see tips in Chapter 9).

This 'divide and conquer' approach is something that you're probably quite good at already. To illustrate, imagine that your classmates have invited you to join them in working in Seattle for the summer. How will you travel to Seattle if there's no direct flight between it and your home city? The obvious way to solve this travel problem is to break the question into a series of smaller tasks or 'sub-goals'. Research shows that this strategy – called **'means-end analysis'** – is widely used by expert problem solvers in every field (Reisberg, 2016). To use this approach, you compare your current situation with your desired goal and then concentrate on reducing the distance between them. In other words, you minimise the gap between where you are now and where *you'd like to be*. The major benefit of this strategy is that it enables you to make progress on your assignment every time you sit down to work on it. You are tackling the problem on your own terms or, in the words of Usain Bolt, *running your own race*.

Find some interest and meaning in every study session you engage in

Flick though your book or notes to see if you can find something that might capture your interest or that has a personal meaning for you. If that proves difficult, setting specific goals for a study session should also work. Remember from Chapter 2 that goal-setting boosts motivation and concentration. To avoid aimlessness, you need to set specific goals every time you study (see practical tips on SMART goal-setting in Chapter 2). In addition, asking yourself 'How can I apply this knowledge to myself?' helps you to remember what you have learned (see Box 1.4).

Use trigger words to re-focus your mind regularly

As our attention span is very short, we can easily get side-tracked during our study sessions. One way of counteracting this problem is to use 'trigger words' to re-focus regularly while studying. For example, a short but vivid verbal reminder such as the word 'relevant?' could serve as shorthand for 'Is this material relevant to my question?' and 'link?' could be used for 'How does this information relate to what I already know?'

Practise mindful awareness

Mindfulness training helps you become more aware of and pay specific attention to your experiences in the present moment, particularly by focusing on breathing. It can also improve your ability to learn (Creswell, 2017). For a practical introduction to mindfulness, try the exercise in Box 6.3.

Box 6.3 Mindful relaxation: Take a one-minute breather

Mindfulness training is a meditative technique that teaches people to develop a moment-to-moment awareness of their own mental states and surroundings. Here is a mindful breathing exercise that you can practise while sitting down in a quiet place before you study. It takes only one minute. If you like, you can ask a friend to read the instructions to you.

1 Sit down on a straight-backed chair with your feet flat on the floor and close your eyes.

2 Lower your shoulders gently and place your hands flat on your thighs.

3 Focus on your breath as it flows in and out of your body. Notice the different sensations that you experience with every breath in . . . and with every breath out. Notice how slowly and deeply you're breathing. There is no need to do anything else – just observe the regularity of your breathing. In and out. In and out.

4 After a while, your mind will wander, but that's fine. Your thoughts will come and go like clouds floating across the sky. Don't try to control these thoughts – just observe them as they arise and float away. Keep focusing on your breathing.

5   Your mind may soon become calm – but if it doesn't, don't worry. Accept whatever happens. And remember, keep focusing on your breathing.

6   After a minute, open your eyes again and you will feel refreshed.

(Adapted from Williams & Penman, 2011)

Mental rehearsal of effective study behaviour

Research in psychology shows that mental rehearsal, or simulating an action in your imagination before actually executing it, can improve both concentration and performance (Moran & Toner, 2017). That's why racing driver Sebastian Vettel, a four-time Formula One world champion, closes his eyes and 'sees' and 'feels' himself driving in his mind's eye before a competition. Mental rehearsal helps him to clear his mind and 'be in the moment' (cited in Brolin, 2017, p. 44). The likely reason for this 'mental practice' effect is that imagined and executed actions rely on partially over-lapping brain processes and neural circuits for their implementation. Applying this technique to your studies, you could imagine your-self writing down 2–3 questions on a blank sheet of paper and focusing on answers to specific questions.

Box 6.4 Using mental rehearsal as a concentration technique

Here is a simple mental rehearsal exercise designed to help you to imagine focusing effectively during a study session. Make sure that you're sitting in a comfortable position, free from distractions. Now read through the instructions two or three times and then close your eyes and see if you can imagine what it asks you to do.

Try to empty your mind of all distractions using the mindfulness exercise in Box 6.3. Now, imagine sitting at your study desk with your pen, paper, laptop and textbooks in front of you. You've allowed yourself plenty of time to study. Try to see yourself writing down a specific question on a blank sheet of paper. You feel excited at the prospect of finding answers to that question. With this question in mind, imagine opening one of your books and flicking through the pages – forward and backwards – making relevant notes. Can you feel yourself stopping as you come across a word or diagram that you don't understand and looking it up on your laptop? When you're finished making your summary notes, you see yourself putting away your textbook and checking that you understand what you've written. You're happy with your progress because you've got some useful notes in front of you.

You could also use mental rehearsal to prepare for a presentation (see also Chapter 9). Try to 'see' and 'feel' this situation in your mind's eye. Visualise all the actions that you wish to perform. For example, imagine speaking slowly and confidently to your class, illustrating ideas using your slides, and answering questions. Notice how calm and confident you are in this situation.

SUMMARY

Concentration, or the ability to focus on what is most important in any situation while ignoring distractions, is a vital skill in everyday life. Unfortunately, most of us are more familiar with lapses of attention than with those rare moments of intense absorption when there is no difference between what we are thinking and what we are doing. How often have you found yourself reading the same sentence in a book again and again because your mind is miles away rather than having a focused state of mind? Therefore, this chapter explored such questions as: *What is concentration? Why do we lose it so easily? What practical techniques can we use to improve our ability to focus more effectively in academic situations?*

In the first section, I likened concentration to a mental spotlight that we shine at things in which we are interested. Your spotlight can be broad or narrow. It's broad when you notice noise and movement as you enter a classroom or lecture theatre. But it's narrow when you listen carefully to your professor giving a lecture. Furthermore, your mental spotlight can shine inwards, such as during a daydream, or outwards, when you're looking at the slides on the screen in class. Although you can't really 'lose' your concentration because your mental spotlight has to shine somewhere, you *can* allow it to be diverted to an irrelevant target – which is exactly what happens when you're distracted. Distractions can be external (e.g. checking your email while you're supposed to be studying) or internal (e.g. planning a social event in your head while sitting in a lecture).

Next, I provided some practical tips on overcoming everyday digital distractions. For example, I mentioned the importance of turning off your notifications while you study.

Finally, I presented six practical techniques which can improve your concentration and help you to study more efficiently. These techniques involved:

1 Establishing study routines

2 Breaking up your study task (means-end analysis)

3 Finding some interest or meaning in every study session

4 Using trigger words to re-focus regularly

5 Practising mindful awareness

6 Mentally rehearsing effective study behaviour.

THINKING IS NATURAL, BUT UNFORTUNATELY, CRITICAL THINKING IS NOT.

Walsh & Paul (1986)

Chapter 7

Learning to Think Critically

Being Sceptical of What You Hear and Read

INTRODUCTION

In August 2017, a group of distinguished professors from Harvard, Princeton and Yale wrote an open letter to students who were about to begin university life. It contained a simple yet inspirational message: 'Think for yourself' (see full text in Bloom et al., 2017). But what does this advice really mean? And why is it so important for students like you? Well, paraphrasing Bloom and his academic colleagues, thinking for yourself has two related meanings. On the one hand, it means *questioning dominant ideas*, especially when other people insist that such ideas are unquestionable. On the other hand, it means *deciding* what you believe – not by conforming slavishly to popular opinions but by forming *independent* conclusions based on a rational evaluation of available evidence and arguments, a task which takes considerable time and mental effort. In their letter, Bloom and his co-authors argue that *critical* thinking is the most important cognitive skill that you can learn in university. This is so, they claim, because the main purpose of a university education is to become a 'lifelong truth-seeker'. Critical thinking is essential for that mission, especially in an era of fake news, spurious claims and opinions masquerading as facts. But there's another reason why critical thinking is important: it's practical and useful and is associated with wise decision making in life. Research by Butler, Pentoney, & Bong (2017) found that critical thinking ability was a better predictor than intelligence of the likelihood of avoiding a range of unwanted life events such as incurring credit card debt and acquiring sexually transmitted diseases. But how can you learn to think critically? The present chapter will answer this question.

This chapter is organised as follows:

....

- ➤ I'll explain 'thinking' as a general mental skill by which we make sense of things.
- ➤ I'll explore what critical thinking involves – namely, a combination of a sceptical attitude with a toolbox of reasoning skills.
- ➤ I'll show you how to use a checklist of critical thinking questions to evaluate whatever claims and arguments you come across in your studies.

....

THINKING: THE SKILL OF MAKING SENSE OF THINGS

We are born to make sense of the world, including other people and ourselves. Early in our lives, we do this by imitation. For example, if you peer into the cot of a newborn infant and stick your tongue out, the baby will usually respond by sticking his or her tongue out too (Gazzaniga, 2018). This imitation shows that infants try to make sense of other people's actions by *simulating* them in their brains – using their imagination to experience and mimic these actions themselves (see also mental rehearsal in Chapter 6). Later, when we learn to speak, we try to resolve gaps in our knowledge by asking questions of everyone we meet. Then, when we go to school and learn to read and write, we use books and electronic media to enrich our understanding by exploring other people's knowledge and experience. As we expand our minds, writing helps us to clarify our own thinking by 'externalising' it. As the novelist E. M. Forster once remarked, 'How can I tell what I think *until I see what I say*?' (my italics). But what exactly happens in our minds when we engage in the mental skill of thinking?

For psychologists, thinking is a mental ('cognitive') process by which we use our knowledge and imagination to go beyond what is immediately obvious in order to see how things could be different. For example, look around the room you're in right now. The fact that you notice that there's furniture in the room doesn't really qualify as thinking – it's just awareness. But imagining what your room would look like if your furniture were *re-arranged* involves a cognitive leap beyond the obvious (Markman & Gentner, 2001), a leap which constitutes thinking. Thinking enables us to transform a situation mentally – to play around with it in our heads. How do we create such mental scenarios? The short answer is: by applying our knowledge. In other words, thinking is what happens when we use what we know or can imagine to transform a situation in our heads.

If you'd like to experience such a transformation first-hand, please try the exercise in Box 7.1. As you will see, the task involves restructuring the elements of a problem so that a solution can emerge, or using your imagination to look at a problem differently. But in what sense is this type of thinking *skilful*?

Box 7.1 Creative thinking: Restructuring a problem

Creative thinkers are highly skilled at rapidly restructuring problems in their minds. To illustrate, what is the sum of all whole numbers between 1 and 1,000?

The obvious (and long-winded) way to solve this problem is to write down all the numbers from 1 to 1,000 and add them up. Although this solution works, it's time-consuming and susceptible to error. Fortunately, there is a much simpler way of tackling this task – a strategy which was discovered after a moment's creative thought by a young mathematical genius called Carl Friedrich Gauss who was presented with this problem by his teacher in school. Here is what happened:

Step 1
Gauss began by writing down the numbers on his paper in the conventional way: $1 + \ldots + 1,000$

Step 2
Then, he looked at the problem again and noticed an unusual pattern: the first number (1) added to the last number (1,000) makes 1,001. The second number (2) added to the penultimate number (999) makes 1,001 … and so on. There are 500 such pairs in the sequence.

$$1 + 2 + 3 + \ldots + 998 + 999 + 1{,}000 = ?$$
$$(1 + 1{,}000) + (2 + 999) + (3 + 998) + \ldots + (500 + 501) = ?$$
$$500(1{,}001) = ?$$

Step 3

Having restructured the problem in his head, he triumphantly announced the solution to his teacher: 500, 500!

Most people agree that physical activities such as tennis and driving are skills because they involve learned behaviour that can be improved through instruction and practice. But how could a mental activity like thinking be regarded as a skill? Well, if we define a skill as any action – physical or mental – which is goal-directed, organised and acquired through training and practice (Annett, 1991), then thinking could be deemed a skilful activity – a view that may be traced back to Bartlett (1958). If thinking is the skill of making sense of things, what exactly is *critical* thinking?

WHAT IS CRITICAL THINKING?

Every day, we are faced with a variety of complex and controversial questions. For example, do people have the right to choose to end their lives? Should certain drugs be legalised? What is the optimal age of digital consent? Unfortunately, as the task of weighing up the evidence on these questions takes a lot of mental effort, we look for shortcuts like relying on our intuition (but see the weaknesses of intuitive thinking in Box 7.6) or else uncritically accepting other people's opinions on the issue. In this passive and 'mindless' state, we resemble sponges because we soak up knowledge indiscriminately (see also Chapter 4).

This blunting of our questioning skills is exacerbated by certain design flaws in our minds. For example, our working memory system is brief and fragile. Unless we deliberately repeat the name of someone we've just been introduced to, it will be forgotten in less than 30 seconds (see also Chapter 8). We find conditional reasoning (or 'if-then' logic) particularly difficult to understand. One way of bypassing these limitations, however, is to systematically question things. As you can see from Box 7.2, different types of questions activate different types of mental processes.

Box 7.2 Asking questions to promote critical thinking

Question	Mental process activated
What are the key features of …?	Analysis and clarification
What is the main assumption underlying …?	Analysis and clarification
What are the strengths and weaknesses of …?	Evaluation
What do you already know about …?	Activating prior knowledge
In what ways are X and Y similar?	Analogical thinking
What do you think would happen if …?	Prediction
What is the evidence to support …?	Analysis and clarification
What is a good example of …?	Application
What is the key idea of …?	Analysis and clarification
Can you think of another way of looking at …?	Creativity

Using questions such as those in Box 7.2 promotes a mental sharpness which underlies all forms of critical thinking. But what exactly does this term mean?

Critical thinking is a form of intelligent criticism that helps people to reach independent and justifiable conclusions about their experiences. According to Gazzaniga, it's the ability 'to systematically question and evaluate information using well-supported evidence (p. G-2, 2018). What makes this form of thinking especially valuable is that it is based on **active reflection** (i.e. working things out for yourself) rather than on passive reproduction of other people's ideas.

To illustrate: when my brother, Dermot, was six years old, he came home one day and informed my mother that he had severe doubts about his teacher's competence. Naturally, my mother was amused by this observation and probed the reason for it. 'Well,' Dermot replied, 'he gave us a spelling test today and told us to close our books – but he kept *his* book open, so he mustn't have known the spellings himself!' Although Dermot's conclusion was not the only one warranted by the evidence available, there is no doubt that he showed the ability to think critically about an everyday situation.

In general, critical thinking involves two key components – a sceptical attitude or disposition and a toolbox of reasoning skills.

The attitudinal part of critical thinking consists of a willingness to question what you learn. That may be difficult for you for personal reasons. For example, you may feel uncomfortable about challenging the views of researchers who are older, better qualified and more knowledgeable than you. But professors expect questions from students because such feedback shows interest and curiosity. Nevertheless, questioning on its own does not guarantee critical thinking. To master this skill, you also need to be able to assess the plausibility of the answers that you hear or read. Therefore, the second component of critical thinking is the ability to spot errors and inconsistencies in the claims, evidence and arguments that are presented to you.

HOW TO IMPROVE YOUR ABILITY TO THINK CRITICALLY: DEVELOPING AMIABLE SCEPTICISM

Although learning to think for yourself has long been championed as a major goal of university education (Dewey, 1933), little or no concern has been devoted to practical ways of improving this skill. This neglect is partly due to a widespread, if mistaken, belief that effective thinking will develop as a spontaneous by-product of learning subjects like computing or mathematics. In other words, teaching people *what* to think will help them in *how* to think well. Unfortunately, there is little evidence to support this assumption.

However, a more direct approach to teaching thinking skills does exist. It's based on encouraging people to ask different types of questions in order to elicit different ways of thinking about things. By asking such questions, you become systematically inquisitive or sceptical. Scepticism, which comes from the Greek word *skeptomai* (which means 'I consider thoughtfully'), is the essence of critical thinking. In exploring this idea, Gazzaniga proposed that the hallmark of a critical thinker is 'amiable scepticism' (p. 5), a trait which combines open-mindedness and wariness.

What specific questions should you ask yourself in order to think critically about something that you hear or read? The following guidelines are based on checklists proposed by Browne & Keeley (2014) and Shermer (1997).

1. What exactly is the claim or conclusion that I am asked to believe?

The first step in critical thinking is to identify the claim or conclusion that you are asked to believe. This task is usually quite easy because authors often *tell you explicitly* what the 'take home' message is by including this information in the subtitle, preface or conclusion of their work. For example, Ericsson & Pool's (2017) book *Peak: How All of Us Can Achieve Extraordinary Things* condenses its main message in the subtitle.

But what if the conclusion isn't stated explicitly? In this case, you will have to infer it from the text. Sometimes this task can be difficult. For example, in everyday life, consider how advertisers manage to overcome the prohibition on making false statements in their publicity by encouraging you to draw conclusions that support their claims. If you were told that 'nine out of ten doctors recommend the pain-killing ingredient in Hangover Tablets', should you conclude that these tablets are effective? Not necessarily. Why? Because the advertisers have neglected to inform you that the same ingredient is common to most pain-killing tablets. In other words, the advertisers' medical endorsement is for the *generic ingredient* – not for the new tablets.

2. Who or what is the source of the claim(s)?

When assessing a claim or an argument, it's important to establish the credibility of the source. Remember, not all information sources are equally trustworthy or impartial. Be cautious about accepting the claims of people who lack verifiable expertise in the topic that they're talking or writing about. Also, be sceptical of people who may endorse something purely for financial gain, such as social media influencers. Likewise, you should be sceptical of research reports commissioned by organisations that possess a vested interest in certain conclusions. It is reasonable to be wary of reports from tobacco companies claiming that smoking cigarettes is harmless.

As well as questioning source credibility, you should be aware of the dangers of over-reliance on second-hand information. A variety of biases and distortions can occur when the 'facts' of a story are dependent on secondary sources. For example, consider the prevalence of urban myths in our lives. These myths are fictitious stories, usually carrying a moral message, which are related as allegedly true events. Typical characters in these stories are cats in microwaves, mysterious hitchhikers and burglars who terrorise babysitters! Interestingly, these stories are found in all cultures and have criss-crossed the globe for many years. One such apocryphal tale concerns a philosophy examination in which a student, when presented with the question 'Why . . . ?' simply wrote down 'Why not?' and allegedly got full marks!

Despite their dubious origins, myths can become a part of scientific folklore. Consider the case of 'subliminal advertising' or the presentation of messages which, although below the threshold of our conscious awareness, may be registered by our minds. Many people have some vague knowledge of research in the US that purported to show that subliminal messages like 'eat popcorn' or 'buy Coke' could unwittingly affect the behaviour of cinema audiences exposed to them. However, there is no evidence that such research was ever conducted (see Lilienfeld et al., 2009). This story became an urban myth simply because it was 'too good to be false'! Two popular 'neuromyths' are described in Box 7.3.

Box 7.3 10 per cent brain use and preferred learning styles: Dispelling pervasive neuromyths

---

The past decade has witnessed an almost exponential growth of research in **neuroscience** – the study of how brain systems give rise to mental processes. But when research on such a complex topic permeates popular discourse, certain inaccuracies are inevitable. 'Neuromyths' are misconceptions generated by a misunderstanding, a misreading or a misquoting of research evidence on how the brain is involved in learning (Dekker et al. 2012). Two of the most common of these myths are the claims that people use only about 10 per cent of their brains and that students learn best when information is tailored to their preferred learning style. Let's consider these myths separately.

The suggestion that we use only '10 per cent of our brains' is intriguing for several reasons. Firstly, it has been popularised for almost 80 years in books (e.g. the foreword to Dale Carnegie's best-selling *How to Win Friends and Influence People* in 1936) and popular media (e.g. Luc Besson's 2014 film, *Lucy*). Secondly, the claim is ambiguous and probably untestable (McBurney, 2002). Finally, and perhaps most significantly, there is little or no evidence to support it (Beyerstein, 1999).

On the one hand, it could mean that we can do without 90 per cent of our brains. Alternatively, it may indicate that we could do 10 times better in mental tasks if we tried harder. However, current neuroscientific research suggests that vast areas of the brain are active during the performance of even the most trivial of mental tasks. Why is this '10 per cent myth' so pervasive and persistent? Perhaps its enduring appeal stems from our willingness to believe that all of us have talents that remain untapped — a vast reservoir of potential that could transform our lives with the right amount of effort.

Another popular and enduring myth concerns 'style-based' instruction — the proposition that people learn best when they receive information in their preferred sensory modality or 'learning style' (e.g. visually if they are 'visual learners' and aurally if they're 'auditory learners'). Again, despite its intuitive appeal, this claim is not supported by scientific evidence (see review by Pashler et al., 2008). For example, Husmann & O'Loughlin (2018) asked over 400 undergraduates on an anatomy course to take a popular online measure of their hypothetical learning style. These participants were also required to adopt the study tips and practices (from the same online site) that were consistent with their dominant learning style.

Results showed that most students did not study in a way that was consistent with their dominant learning style. Perhaps more importantly, those students who aligned their study habits with their preferred learning style did not achieve better end-of-year anatomy grades than did counterparts who didn't match their studies with their style. Husmann & O'Loughlin (2018) concluded that, although students seemed to be interested in their learning styles, many of them didn't actually change their studying behaviour based on them. Even if they had done so, it probably wouldn't have made any difference to their grades. In conclusion, just as in the case of subliminal advertising, the learning-style claim is popular because it is 'too good to be false'!

In order to counteract distortions arising from the biasing effect of second-hand information, Gilovich (1991) recommended that your scepticism should be in direct proportion to the remoteness of the source of the claim in question. In other words, the more distant the source, the less credible the story that emanates from it. Accordingly, whenever possible, you should consult **primary sources** (i.e. the original book or article by a certain author) in order to validate claims encountered in **secondary sources** such as textbooks.

3. What evidence is used to support the main argument or central claim(s)?

The information that bombards us every day stems from a variety of sources ranging from intuitive hunches or gut reactions to controlled laboratory experiments. Not all of these sources of information are equally trustworthy. A major problem with insights yielded by intuitive impressions is that they are invariably based on a limited sample of experience. Thus, a single media report of a spectacular airplane crash might cause you to overestimate the danger of travelling by air – even though, statistically, you may be much more likely to die in a car crash. In fact, travelling by car is about *100 times* more dangerous than is travelling by plane (Lennox, 2018).

A list of some common sources of evidence that you may encounter in your studies is presented in Box 7.4.

Box 7.4 Common sources of evidence cited in arguments

Intuition (gut feeling): 'Deep down, I know that ...'

A private feeling or hunch which may be used both to make and to justify judgements and decisions.

Appeal to authority: 'According to Professor Smith ...'

Ascribing a claim, a quotation or an argument to an apparently prestigious source or expert authority in an effort to enhance its credibility or persuasive appeal.

Anecdotal evidence: 'Someone I know ...'

Includes reference to personal experiences such as observations, case studies or examples.

Research evidence: 'Studies show that ...'

Comprises data obtained through systematic, objective and repeatable procedures (e.g. a controlled laboratory experiment).

Although space limitations preclude a detailed analysis of these types of evidence, the use of case studies deserves special attention. For example, critics of the legal system may try to highlight the inequities of sentencing policy by presenting vivid examples of offenders who have received disproportionately severe punishments for petty crimes. Although such case studies can provide compelling insights that resonate with our experience, they are highly selective in nature and hence susceptible to many biases. How can we be sure that the case study is representative of the population from which it comes? When we encounter a case study, we should be careful to ask questions about sampling, generalisability and the possible existence of any counter examples that may challenge the conclusions presented to us.

4. How valid is the evidence cited? Identifying weaknesses in people's arguments and claims

Having identified the foundations of the statements being presented as facts, the next step is to *evaluate* this evidence systematically. This task is very important as you will be expected to become a shrewd and efficient consumer of research information in university. This means that you will have to become adept at identifying weaknesses in people's arguments and claims. To help you with this, here are some questions to ask (see also Sinnott-Armstrong & Foegelin, 2010).

Is the claim based on accurate information?

A claim may be based on inaccurate information. For example, consider the widespread belief that spinach is unusually rich in iron. This belief is mistaken, as research suggests that there is more iron in eggs, liver, brown sugar or pulses than in spinach (Skrabanek & McCormick, 1989). This myth arose from research conducted in the late 1890s and served as a useful propaganda weapon for the Allied Forces during Second World War when meat was rationed. Indeed, according to Hamblin (1981), evidence has existed since the 1930s to show that the original researchers who investigated the iron content of spinach put the decimal point in the wrong place, thereby overestimating the resulting value tenfold! Although this latter suggestion may *itself* be apocryphal (Ramsey, 2017), it highlights the importance of seeking evidence to support our beliefs.

Is the reasoning valid?
Another common flaw afflicting arguments arises from invalid reasoning processes. Imagine you are a scientist who has received criticism for your theory that extrasensory perception (ESP) exists. In a public debate on this topic, you produce the following argument: Pasteur's idea that diseases were transmitted by microscopic germs was dismissed as false during his lifetime. This has since been accepted as true. Therefore, since your theory has also been ridiculed by the scientific community, then your theory must, in fact, be true. Is this argument valid? Of course it isn't, but it could convince some people that your ideas are correct.

Are the assumptions valid?
One weakness of many arguments concerns shaky foundations or questionable assumptions. This problem is especially likely when figurative language is used because metaphors always carry implicit assumptions with them when they are imported into arguments or theories. For example, the traditional metaphor of seeing the long-term memory system as a container is flawed because a container can be filled beyond its capacity and can overflow. Although this model seems intuitively plausible, research shows that there is no known capacity limit to our long-term memory. In short, the more we know, the more we can remember!

Does the argument 'beg the question' or assume its own answer?
A fourth flaw in an argument arises when it 'begs the question' or takes its own conclusion for granted. For example, consider the proposition that 'Telepathy exists because I have had a number of experiences in my life I would describe as telepathic'. This proposition begs the question because its conclusion ('telepathy exists')

is based on evidence that requires you to *already accept* that the claim is true.

Here's another example of this fallacy (taken from Forshaw, 2012). Imagine hearing a teacher addressing a parents' meeting with the words: 'As a mother myself, I know a lot about child development.' Where is the evidence that being a mother equips one with a lot of knowledge about child development? As Forshaw (2012) pointed out, 'being something, or possessing something, does not give you *a priori* unquestionable expertise on the subject. That must be proved elsewhere.' (p. 14)

Sometimes, spurious reasoning about the possession of specialist knowledge can backfire spectacularly. For example, a controversial claim about motherhood caused a political furore in the UK in 2016 during a contest for the leadership of the Conservative party. One of the candidates, Andrea Leadsom, had to apologise to her rival, Theresa May, for a comment in which she implied that being a mother gave her 'a real stake in the future of our country' – unlike May, who does not have children. A popular and damaging inference from Leadsom's remark was that May, and other childless people, don't care what happens to the UK. Clearly, the claim that being a parent as a qualifying characteristic for running a country is nonsensical (Brockwell, 2016). Not surprisingly, Leadsom resigned from the leadership race in the wake of her ill-judged remark.

Evaluating evidence

In summary, all sources of evidence have their limitations. Therefore, you might find it helpful to examine Box 7.5 so that you will know what to look for when you are required to evaluate evidence in your subject.

Let's look at some of the sources of evidence described in Box 7.5. Perhaps the most frequently used one is the 'appeal to authority'. Here, testimonials or endorsements may be given by people who are acknowledged authority figures in a particular field. For example, a leading heart surgeon or world-class athlete may be quoted on the cardiovascular benefits of regular exercise. But should we readily accept what these eminent people have said about this topic? Well, as critical thinkers, we should immediately look for evidence to support any conclusions which we are offered. To do this, we should check whether or not the expert involved has any specialist knowledge in the field in question. For example, a Nobel Prize-winner's views on her or his subject are presumably better informed than those of somebody unknown in this field. However, if no evidence is adduced to support this person's position, or if the expert's pronouncement lies outside her or his domain of expertise (a trick that is exploited repeatedly in advertising), then her or his opinions must be treated with scepticism. Always be wary of what information you trust online. For tips on assessing the reliability of websites, see Chapter 4.

Box 7.5 How good is the evidence? What to look out for when evaluating explanations

---

Source	Potential flaw
Intuition	Inaccessible to public scrutiny and hence unverifiable.
Personal experience	Personal observations ('I saw it with my own eyes') or single episodes, no matter how vivid, do not constitute proof. They are also subject to distortions arising from biases in memory.
Expert authority	The 'expert' involved may be commenting on a topic outside her or his specialist field (in which case, the opinion offered is questionable) or she or he may be doing so for personal gain (in which case, the opinion is biased).
Case studies	Examples do not constitute proof. They are also susceptible to selection biases (only picking ones that support your argument). The absence of relevant comparative data makes interpretation of case studies difficult.
Research evidence	Difficult and time-consuming to obtain – but the most powerful evidence as it is based on systematic, empirical methods.

5. Are there alternative explanations for the evidence provided? If so, how plausible are these rival theories?

What you see depends on the view from where you are standing. In other words, there are always alternative ways of interpreting anything. Indeed, the possibility of identifying rival explanations for an agreed set of circumstances is the cornerstone of our legal system. If a defence counsel can prove that there is at least a 'reasonable doubt' about her or his client's involvement in a crime, then the case against this person may be dismissed. By implication, if you can establish an interpretation of the evidence that is at least as plausible as that favoured by the theorist, then you have shown a capacity to think for yourself. Remember, it is this ability to think rigorously that is the hallmark of a First Class Honours answer from a student.

To illustrate the search for 'rival causes', consider the mystery of 'out of the body' (OBE) experiences. These phenomena, which are commonly reported in certain situations, particularly when one is close to death, refer to changes in consciousness that are accompanied by a feeling that one's centre of awareness has shifted to a position that is separate from one's body. One possible explanation for these experiences is that they prove the existence of the soul. This is a supernatural explanation of the known facts. However, alternative explanations are possible – natural ones that are compatible with known physical or psychological principles.

A good place to start looking for what causes certain phenomena is to analyse the situations in which these phenomena occur. In the case of OBEs, the vast majority of them are reported when people are lying down in a state of reverie, between wakefulness and sleep, on a bed or in an operating theatre. When people are lying down in a relaxed state, several things can happen. Firstly, being stationary for long periods of time can cause habituation (or shutting off) of the receptors that regulate our body sense. As a result, we may experience a sensation of floating. Secondly, research shows that the incidence of OBEs is about three times higher in patients with vestibular problems (e.g. difficulties in balancing properly) than in healthy people (Zhang, 2017). This finding suggests that OBEs may be caused by a mismatch between the information provided to the brain by a damaged vestibular system and a normal visual system. These two neuroscientific explanations of OBEs challenge the assumption that such phenomena offer unequivocal proof of the existence of souls.

6. Check your assumptions before drawing conclusions

The final step in learning to think critically is to make sure that you check your assumptions before drawing any conclusions. Unfortunately, our desire to solve problems quickly sometimes leads us into error. To test your assumption-checking skills, please try the exercise in Box 7.6. As you will discover, Box 7.6 reveals the folly of taking things for granted. Taking things for granted is the antithesis of critical thinking because it's rooted in passivity rather than in active questioning.

Box 7.6 Check your assumptions: How good are you at solving puzzles?

Problem 1: The bat and ball problem (adapted from Kahneman, 2011)

A bat and a ball cost €1.10 in total. The bat costs €1 more than the ball. How much does the ball cost?

Problem 2: Number sequence problem

Why are these numbers arranged in the following sequence?

$$8, 5, 4, 9, 1, 7, 6, 3, 2, 0$$

Problem 3: Bus driver problem

Imagine that you are a bus driver. At the first stop, 3 men and 2 women get on. At the second stop, 1 man and 4 women get on. At the third stop, 2 men and 3 women get on and 2 women get off. How old is the bus driver?

The answers to these puzzles are on pp 122–3.

Overall, this section presented a set of questions and techniques that are intended to promote intelligent criticism of the information that bombards you every day. Let us now summarise this advice as a practical checklist for your role as a research 'consumer' in the university.

PUTTING IT ALL TOGETHER: BECOMING A CRITICAL READER

During your studies at university, you will be expected to read thousands of books and articles, all of which will try to convince you of the merit of their authority, information or arguments. How can you apply the critical thinking skills that you have learned in this chapter to evaluate this literature thoroughly? Here are some practical guidelines in this regard.

- Who are the authors? Do they have verifiable and relevant expertise in their field?

- What is the main 'take home' message of the book or article? What specific claims or ideas are they asking you to believe?

- What type of evidence do the authors cite in support of their conclusion? See Box 7.4.

- Is this evidence valid and convincing? Are there any alternative explanations for the evidence supplied by the author?

- Has this book or paper been evaluated critically by other researchers? You can get this information by checking citations of the book or paper in databases relevant to your subject.

- How do the authors' ideas and findings fit in with what you already know?

SUMMARY

Thinking is the skill of making sense of things. It seems so natural and effortless that you can easily take it for granted. But certain kinds of thinking require both mental effort and special training. One such skill is *critical thinking* or the ability to question things systematically, evaluate information and reach independent conclusions using well-supported evidence. For many academics, this skill is crucial for happiness and success in university. In short, the ability to think critically (to 'think for yourself') is the hallmark of an educated mind. But what does critical thinking involve and how can you develop this skill? The present chapter attempted to answer these questions.

- I began by proposing that thinking is a mental skill by which we make sense of the world (including ourselves and other people).

- Then, I explained that *critical* thinking is a form of intelligent criticism that helps us to reach independent and rationally justifiable conclusions about what we hear or read. It has two key components:

  ◦ The first one is an open-minded yet sceptical attitude ('amiable scepticism') that encourages you to question any claims or conclusions that you are asked to accept.

  ◦ The second component is a 'toolbox' of reasoning skills that allow you to evaluate the validity of the evidence and arguments that you encounter.

- Having given you some practical tips on improving each of these elements of critical thinking, I presented a brief checklist of questions designed to help you to become a critical reader.

Answer to Box 7.6

A great deal of what we know about people's difficulties in thinking comes from psychological research using specially designed puzzles (e.g. see Kahneman, 2011). Typically, these puzzles (see Box 7.6) induce us to make false assumptions or to focus on irrelevant information, both of which hamper critical evaluation of the information available. Although research papers are not written to mislead you, they do not always convey their assumptions explicitly. Therefore, you must always ask questions like 'What are we assuming here?' and 'What information is relevant and what is irrelevant?' in order to become a more critical and discerning consumer of research information.

Answer to 'bat and ball' problem

For many people, the obvious answer is that the ball costs 10 cent. Is this what you came up with?

That's the answer that more than 50 per cent of students at Harvard, Princeton and MIT gave when faced with this puzzle

(Kahneman, 2011) – but it's wrong! If the ball costs 10 cent and the bat costs €1 more than the ball, then the bat would cost €1.10 for a grand total of €1.20. The correct answer to this problem is that the ball costs 5 cent and the bat costs – at €1 more – €1.05, thereby making a grand total of €1.10.

Why do so many of us get his problem wrong? (Kahneman estimated that it could be as high as 80 per cent of people!) The answer seems to lie in a combination of laziness (avoidance of a few seconds of mental effort) and an overreliance on intuition. A curious feature of the latter issue is that people who answer wrongly have missed an important social cue: why would anyone pose a puzzle with such an obvious answer?

Another explanation for mistakes with this puzzle is that people often substitute difficult problems with simpler ones in order to solve them quickly. In this puzzle, they may unconsciously substitute the 'more than' statement (the bat costs €1.00 *more than* the ball) with an absolute statement (the bat costs €1.00). This makes the calculations much easier to work with in your head. If a ball and bat together cost €1.10 and the bat costs €1.00, then the ball must cost 10 cent. In this case, simplifying the question leads to an incorrect answer.

Answer to number sequence problem

The answer is: the numbers are arranged in alphabetical order – 8 (eight), 5 (five), 4 (four), 9 (nine), 1 (one), 7 (seven), 6 (six), 3 (three), 2 (two), 0 (zero).

Many people find this series problem difficult because they make an understandable, but false, assumption that the solution lies in the *numerical* relationship between the items. The numbers in the series encourage you to adopt a numerical or **'mental set'** way of looking at things based on past experience (Luchins, 1942). However, by asking yourself 'Is there another way of looking at these items?' you may discover that the items represent words rather than numbers. The lesson is clear: when facing problems, we need to check the validity of our assumptions.

Answer to the bus driver problem

Remember that *you* are the bus driver so your age is the correct answer. The information about passenger numbers is irrelevant to the solution.

TELL ME AND I FORGET, TEACH ME AND I MAY REMEMBER, INVOLVE ME AND I LEARN.

Chinese proverb

Chapter 8

Remembering and Understanding

Principles and Practical Tips

INTRODUCTION

If you want to become a better learner in any area of life, you need to explore how your brain works in acquiring new knowledge and skills. Therefore, the purpose of this chapter is to provide some scientific principles and practical tips on a key aspect of learning in university: namely, how to improve your ability to remember and understand new information. According to Mayer (2002), we can distinguish between two types of learning tasks: those that involve 'meaningful learning' and those that involve 'rote learning'. Meaningful learning requires abstract thinking in which you try to understand new concepts and ideas and apply them successfully to challenging tasks (e.g. writing a research assignment or preparing a presentation; see Chapter 9). By contrast, rote learning involves memorizing facts such as the periodic table in chemistry or foreign vocabulary in language studies. In university, the vast majority of your learning falls into the 'meaningful' category because it's motivated by a clear and specific purpose: to improve your knowledge and skills in the subjects that you have chosen to study (recall 'active learning' in Chapter 1). How can you improve your memory and understanding?

This chapter is organised as follows:

••

➤ I'll explore the nature, stages and various stores of your memory system.

➤ I'll present some practical strategies for improving your ability to understand new material.

➤ I'll consider certain mnemonics (or practical memory aids) to help you with academic tasks that require rote learning or memorizing information based on repetition.

••

WHAT IS MEMORY?

Memory is a brain process that enables us to store, organise and retrieve a vast amount of information. It contains general knowledge, personal experiences and many different skills and stores them over time so that they're available to us later when required. As you can imagine, without memory, we would not be able to read, write or perform even the simplest of actions because all of these skills depend on our ability to retrieve stored knowledge quickly and accurately. What kind of storage system is our memory? Although human memory has been compared to various mechanical systems and devices, it is unique in its power and flexibility. It is much more sophisticated than a container or filing cabinet because it never fills up. In fact, your memory expands to accommodate new knowledge. As Oliver Wendell Holmes put it, 'One's mind, once stretched by a new idea, never regains its original dimensions.' (Carter, 2012) Thus, the more you know about something of interest to you, the more you will remember about it. In a similar vein, memory is significantly more powerful than electronic playback devices like video cameras. These machines retrieve stored information in a literal and faithful manner: you see what was recorded – no more, no less. By contrast, human memory is 'a fallible process that is inferential and reconstructive – not literal' (Bjork et al., 2013, p. 420). Our minds store interpretations of events, not the actual experiences themselves. Therefore, remembering is a constructive process in which we use prior knowledge and expectations to build an interpretation of what happened in the past.

A crucial implication of this idea is that what we recall of an event is usually a blend of fact and fantasy. Consider the case of

Jean Piaget, the famous developmental psychologist, who had a vivid memory of being kidnapped as a child while under the care of his nanny. Remarkably, he discovered years later that she had fabricated the entire story in order to explain a clandestine meeting with a boyfriend (Piaget, 1962). This revelation means that Piaget must have unwittingly incorporated his nanny's fictitious tale into his own memory and 'experienced' it – even though it *never actually happened.*

Another difference between our minds and mechanical storage systems such as computers concerns the way in which we search our memory. If a computer were asked the question, 'What is Shakespeare's phone number?' it would search its memory files for entries under 'Shakespeare' and 'phone number'. But when we are faced with the same question, we effortlessly apply our general knowledge that phone hadn't been invented in Shakespeare's time before spending any time trying to answer the question. This example also highlights another intriguing feature of human cognition – our minds tend to *speed up* as we acquire more knowledge but computers tend to *slow down* as they store more information.

One reason for this advantage of our memory system over that of a computer is that our brains are *hardwired to make connections:* new information reminds us of things we already know. That's why spacing your study sessions over time (distributed practice; see Box 3.3) works better than cramming. Distributed practice creates more opportunities for your brain to forge neural connections between new information and existing knowledge. As neuroscientists say, brain cells that *wire* together *fire* together!

HOW GOOD IS YOUR MEMORY?

At this stage, I'd like to test your ability to remember some numbers (see Box 8.1). Although this exercise involves a trick, it highlights a crucial principle of memory: the idea that breaking down the information to be learned into smaller, more meaningful units (called 'chunks') improves your memory.

Do you think that you could remember the following ten-digit sequence? 9871916911. This task is very difficult because our short-term memory has only about seven vacant 'slots' for incoming information. In other words, its holding capacity (or 'span') is limited to seven separate items. As ten numbers exceeds that span, it's virtually impossible to recall them accurately. But remembering a ten-digit number becomes much easier if you 'chunk' or break down the sequence into a smaller number of familiar or meaningful units – say, three such units. These could be '987' (counting down from 9), '1916' (a number with links to Irish history) and '911' (associated with the emergency phone number in the US). This sequence is now a lot easier to recall.

Clearly, the more efficiently you can chunk information, the more you can remember. This leads to a key principle of memory – the more you *know*, the more you can *remember*! In this sense, knowledge really is power.

Box 8.1 How good is your memory for numbers?

The purpose of this exercise is to test your memory for a sequence of 24 numbers. Look at the figures for ten seconds. Then, turn away from the page and see how many of them you can recall in the correct sequence.

1 4 9 1 6 2 5 3 6 4 9 6 4 8 1 1 0 0 1 2 1 1 4 4

If you're like most people, you may remember the first few numbers and possibly a few at the end – but almost no number from the middle of the sequence. Now, see if you can find a pattern in the numbers. Here's a hint . . . break them into chunks like this:

1, 4, 9, 16, 25, 36 and so on.

What's the pattern? A clue is 'squared'.

Instead of having to recall 24 separate numbers, all you have to do is to remember one item: the pattern that generates these numbers. Amazingly, knowledge of this pattern will enable you to recall the numbers *backwards* as well as forwards! If you're still baffled, the solution can be found at the end of the chapter.

STAGES OF MEMORY: ENCODING, STORAGE AND RETRIEVAL

What steps do our minds go through when we remember something? Psychologists have identified three stages in this process (see Figure 8.1).

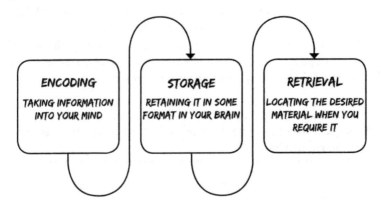

Figure 8.1:The three stages of memory

Encoding

'Encoding' is the process by which your brain takes in and 'encodes' information to create an initial memory trace. A visual code could represent the information as a picture or a mental image, an acoustic code could represent it as a sequence of sounds, or a semantic code could represent it in terms of its meaning. The more codes you use to process information, the more likely you are to remember it. This principle explains why your memory for *faces* is usually better than that for names. Whereas faces can be encoded in two ways (as names or as pictures), names are usually encoded in only one way (as sounds). Also, while other people's faces contain many features that activate our brain such as eyes, expressions or mouth movements, names are typically perceived as being just a series of syllables associated with a face (Burnett, 2017).

But why are names so forgettable? Perhaps the most common reason for forgetting the name of someone you've been introduced to at a party is that you haven't paid sufficient attention to it in the first place. A simple way to overcome this type of encoding failure is to politely ask the person to repeat their name and for you to say it back to them. The double benefit here is that you are not only paying the person the compliment of asking to hear her or his name pronounced correctly but you're also receiving another chance to encode aloud the details that you missed initially.

Semantic encoding, or looking for meaning in something you come across, is especially useful when you're trying to understand a passage of information in a textbook. Asking yourself 'What does this mean?' or 'Can I explain this idea in simpler language?' forces you to make more effort in making sense of the information. In general, encoding problems are best tackled by investing more mental effort in your studies (see Box 8.2).

Box 8.2 Invest more mental effort in your studies and 'overlearn' at the end

---

Mental effort is a crucial prerequisite of effective learning because it enriches the encoding stage of memory. Imagine that you're studying a chapter in a textbook. You can invest more mental effort in this task by asking yourself questions like 'What does this mean?' and 'How could I explain this idea, theory or concept to other students in simpler language?' Many students forget academic material simply because it never 'went in' properly in the first place. In general, there are two practical ways of overcoming this encoding problem: one to use before you begin your studies and the other to use at the end. Ask yourself, 'What exactly do I want to learn in this study session?' before you open your books. If possible, give yourself 2–3 specific study questions for the session (see Chapter 1 for practical tips). After you have finished a block of study, use the strategy of 'overlearning'. This technique involves consolidating what you have learned by *going over it one more time* just to make sure that you understand it fully. Overlearning boosts memory by enhancing your encoding of the information.

Research shows that the more *deeply* you encode information, the more meaningful it is to you (see also Box 1.4) and the richer and more durable will be your memory of it (Craik & Lockhart, 1972). Consider a diagram in one of your textbooks. When you first come across this diagram, you could look at the colours in the picture (shallow processing), read the labels attached to the diagram (deeper processing) or try to find out *what the diagram really means* (deepest level of processing). In general, the last of these encoding strategies (looking for the meaning of the diagram) works best. This principle – that deep processing is the key to understanding – provides a logical foundation for the questioning (Q) part of the PQRR reading strategy (see Box 5.5 for more details).

Storage

After information has been encoded, it has to be stored or represented in your memory as a sound, picture, motor action or another format. A name such as 'Jennifer' could be stored as an auditory pattern of three syllables ('Jen-ni-fer') or as a mental image (a picture of the actress Jennifer Lawrence). But a skill like driving a car requires a different storage format: a motor programme that is compiled through extensive practice. Any storage is enhanced by *repetition* of the information to be learned. Therefore, 'maintenance rehearsal' – or rote repetition – is especially useful for learning a physical skill or even for learning the definition of a new term in a textbook.

'Neural plasticity' or 'neuroplasticity' means 'the ability of the nervous system to change in response to experience or environmental stimulation' (VandenBos, 2015). By repeating this definition to yourself a few times, either in your mind or out loud, you're increasing the likelihood that you'll remember it later. However, if you rush through a difficult passage in a textbook (an unfortunate reading habit of unsuccessful students; see Box 1.3, p. 8), you won't have time to repeat the definition out loud. As a result, you'll miss out on the opportunity to benefit from maintenance rehearsal of the information

Retrieval

Retrieval is the process of accessing or recalling stored information when necessary, such as a fact, experience or skill. Normally, it requires a cue. If someone you know walks towards you on the street, their face usually triggers your memory of their name. Similarly, the rhyme 'Thirty days hath September . . .' serves as a cue to retrieve the number of days in any month. Unfortunately, if you don't practise using retrieval cues when you study, your memory will let you down. Have you ever experienced the 'tip of the tongue' phenomenon? Here, you can't retrieve a word or name even though you *know* that you know it! What's fascinating – and frustrating – about this experience is that you can recall other details of the missing memory ('I know that actor was in film with . . .'). The good news, however, is that the elusive answer usually pops into your mind later – which indicates that memory search processes take place in stages, some of which are unconscious in nature.

Research suggests that our retrieval processes are remarkably *context-dependent* (see also Box 2.5, p. 28). When we learn something, we encode features of the *environment* or context in which the learning occurred as well as the actual material itself. Therefore, people tend to remember information better when their attempted recall takes place in an environment or context that is similar to the one in which the original learning occurred. Evidence to support the context-dependency of memory comes from an ingenious experiment by Godden & Baddeley (1975). These researchers asked scuba divers to learn lists of words in two different environments – on dry land and underwater. One half of the divers learned the words while sitting on the shore whereas the other half learned them while they were underwater (using special communication devices). Later, their memory for these words was tested either in 'congruent' conditions (i.e. in the same environment in which they had originally learned the information) or in 'incongruent' circumstances (i.e. in a different environment). Results showed that, as predicted by the context-dependency effect, the divers *recalled more words* under the *congruent* rather than the incongruent circumstances.

The context-dependency of memory applies to *internal* factors as well as to environmental ones. For example, people's state of mind, influenced by levels of intoxication or mood, can affect their retrieval of information. Thus, Goodwin et al. (1969) found evidence of 'state specific' recall when they investigated the effect of alcohol on people's performance on various memory tasks. Their results showed that what participants had learned when drunk was recalled better when they were drunk than when sober; and what participants had learned when sober was recalled better when in the same state. Interestingly, this principle of the 'state dependency' of memory may explain why a depressed mood is difficult to overcome in everyday life. In this case, the negative mood may facilitate the learning and retrieval of additional negative information in the person's life, thereby prolonging the depressed state of mind (Eysenck & Keane, 2015). Applied to exam preparation, a practical implication of context-dependency retrieval is that you should test your memory for academic material *under exam-like conditions* as often as possible (i.e. in the absence of your books or notes; see also Chapter 10). In summary, research shows that memory performance is influenced by three main factors – the way in which the information is encoded initially, the manner in which it is stored and the type of cues that are used to retrieve it.

MEMORY STORES

People often complain about the frailty of their memory as if it were a single process – but it isn't. We have multiple memory systems, each of which has its distinctive strengths and limitations (Gazzaniga, 2018). According to the standard or 'modal model' (Atkinson & Shiffrin, 1968), memory comprises three stores: sensory memory (SM), short-term memory (STM; but called 'working memory' (WM) in modern models of human memory) and long-term memory (LTM). These stores represent the different 'way stations' though which information flows on its journey from the outside world into the mind.

Sensory memory

Sensory memory is the short-lived retention of sensory information. Have you ever had the experience of asking someone to repeat a sentence that you were only half-listening to – only to discover that you 'heard' an echo of what they said before they repeated it? Research shows that echoes of what you hear and flashes of what you see (Pratte, 2018) linger in your sensory memory for a split second before they vanish. Interestingly, the persistence of visual information in sensory memory is partly responsible for your ability to perceive movement in films despite the fact that what you are actually looking at is a series of static images alternating with blank intervals. If you'd like to experience sensory memory in action, try the exercise in Box 8.3 on the 'rubber pencil' illusion (Pomerantz, 1983).

Box 8.3 Experiencing sensory memory: The rubber pencil illusion

Take a pencil in your right hand. Hold it loosely at the base between your thumb and forefinger (with the point at the top). Now, extend your arm out fully and slowly wiggle the pencil around. Notice how 'rubbery' the pencil appears as it seems to flex conspicuously. This illusion is caused by the fact that your visual sensory memory system (called 'iconic memory') has created a time-lag of up to a second between the actual and perceived position of the pencil in space. Your mind tries to make sense of this disparity by 'seeing' the pencil as flexible or rubbery. According to Gazzaniga (2018), our sensory memory system enables us to experience the world as a continuous stream of information rather than as a series of discrete sensations. For example, when you turn your head, the visual scene passes smoothly in front of you rather than in a jerky manner. Here, your iconic memory holds information for just long enough to enable you to connect one image with the next in a smooth way – one that corresponds to the way in which objects move in the real world.

Unfortunately, the contents of sensory memory decay rapidly. Therefore, only a fraction of the information bombarding your senses is actually transferred to the next stage of the memory system: working memory.

Working memory

In Chapter 6, I explained that working memory is a mental system for holding a small amount of information in mind while we consciously work on it (D'Esposito & Postle, 2015). WM is your thinking memory. The ideas and thoughts in this system are the ones on which you're *currently working*. In everyday life, WM is activated when you check that your change is correct in a shop or when you give or receive spoken directions. It has a very limited capacity (perhaps as few as four items) and its duration is a matter of only 15–30 seconds – unless you actively rehearse the information or action that you're trying to remember. You may also recall from Chapter 6 that when you try to multiply two large numbers in your head (e.g. 39 by 26), your WM becomes overloaded. But to experience a less challenging WM task, try this exercise: imagine standing in front of your house or apartment building. How many windows can you see in your mind's eye? Now, count these windows to yourself. Here, your 'inner eye' (a part of the WM system that controls your ability to manipulate visual and spatial information) allows you to create and inspect a visual image of your house or apartment. At the same time, your 'inner voice' (a part of the WM system that controls your ability to process sounds) enables you to count each of the windows that you can 'see'.

The fact that information can be kept alive in WM through rehearsal leads us to an important point. There are two different types of repetition: 'maintenance' rehearsal and 'elaborative' rehearsal. As I explained earlier, maintenance rehearsal involves the rote repetition of information in an effort to keep it 'alive' in your WM. Unfortunately, as soon as you stop repeating the information, it disappears. Another form of repetition is needed to ensure a more durable retention of information. Elaborative rehearsal involves thinking about what the to-be-remembered items mean and how they're related both to each other and to what you already know. As William James said, 'Our conscious effort should not be so much to *impress* or *retain* [knowledge] as to connect it with something already there.' (1889, p. 143) To summarise, elaborative rehearsal produces deeper encoding of material than does maintenance rehearsal and so leads to better understanding and recall.

Long-term memory
Long-term memory contains everything that we know and can do, most of which you're *not* thinking about at this moment (Reisberg, 2016). It stores vast amounts of knowledge and beliefs (names, dates, rules, skills) for indefinite durations that can range from a few minutes to an entire lifetime. This knowledge includes both factual information and procedural skills such as how to tie your shoelaces. Within LTM, knowledge is dynamically organised in meaningful units called 'schemas', which are mental represen-tations of categories of people, objects and events. We use these

mental structures to make sense of things. For example, in Box 4.3 of Chapter 4 I demonstrated that it's easy to understand and remember an obscure passage of text if you can find the appropriate heading, frame of reference or 'schema' for it.

Evidence of this *semantic* organisation of long-term memory comes from the pattern of mistakes that people tend to make when recalling information from this store. For example, they might say 'ship' instead of 'boat' – indicating that they had stored the word according to its meaning rather than its sound. Since LTM is organised semantically, then the way in which we impose *meaning* on or interpret new information is critical to the accuracy with which we recall it later.

PRACTICAL TECHNIQUES TO IMPROVE UNDERSTANDING AND MEMORY

'Understanding' is the term we use to describe our ability to interpret, explain or impose meaning on things. It is constructed or built up from our use of background knowledge and assumptions in order to draw conclusions about what we hear or see. Consider how we construct an understanding of a piece of text. The text that I've chosen is the opening sentence of Jean-Paul Sartre's existential short story called 'The Wall' (1939), which is set during the Spanish Civil War.

> *They pushed us into a big white room and I began to blink because the light hurt my eyes.* (See text in Hoffman, 2014)

What's going on? Taken literally, the text describes an incident in which the narrator and others were pushed into a large white room. Notice how you use your knowledge and imagination to *go beyond* what you are told explicitly. The fact that the narrator's eyes blinked suggests that she or he had been in a darkened room earlier. Furthermore, the word 'pushed' implies that she or he had left this room involuntarily. The large white room conjures up an impression of a prison or a hospital. Clearly, your 'understanding' of such sentences depends on our ability to 'fill in' the gaps in what you are told by using your knowledge and imagination constructively.

How can you improve your ability to understand things? Psychologists have identified a number of techniques that will improve your understanding of what you wish to learn. These techniques are as follows:

1   Write down 2–3 specific questions about the material to be learned before you read it (depth of processing).

2   Make a special effort to pay attention to the details of the material when you read it first (enhanced encoding).

3   Use headings to organise the material (schematic processing).

4   Try to link the new material to what you already know (elaborative rehearsal).

5   Pause and check that you actually understand what you have read (comprehension monitoring).

6   Test yourself regularly to see what you can remember about what you've been reading (retrieval practice).

7   Form a study group to share and discuss different perspective on the academic material under analysis.

Write down 2–3 specific questions: Use the PQRR technique

According to the depth of processing principle (see Box 8.2), asking questions about the meaning of the material that you are about to learn produces better understanding and subsequent recall than does passive reading of it. Therefore, use the PQRR strategy every time you read a book or set of notes (see Chapter 5 for more details).

Pay attention to the details of the material

To encode information properly, you must make an effort to notice its details. When reading new information, make a special note of the definition and key features of the topic in question. Write these details down on a summary sheet (see also Chapter 5).

Use headings to organise the material

As organisation improves memory and understanding, try to classify or write headings for the information that you wish to learn. For example, do you think that you could make any sense of the following passage of text?

> Selling his jewels, the explorer ignored his rivals' taunts and sneers: 'I will prove you wrong,' he thundered, 'The earth is an egg, not a table.' Surging through the watery expanse, the days became weeks and rumours grew that he had fallen off the edge. But, at last, winged harbingers appeared and circled the explorers, indicating that the quest was over.
>
> Based on an experiment by Dooling & Lachman, 1971

The above passage is almost impossible to understand. Although you know what the individual words mean, you may fail to grasp the overall meaning. Why? Because it lacks a heading or frame of reference that could help you to link it to something you already know. Notice what happens when you are told that the passage is entitled 'Columbus Discovers America'. Armed with this heading, you can activate your existing knowledge about Columbus, which helps you to decipher the meaning of the text. I made a similar point in Chapter 4 when using the passage on washing clothes (see Box 4.3, p. 56). These examples show that *headings* can boost your understanding because they enable you to organise new information and to relate it to what you already know. Headings enhance all three steps in remembering – encoding, storage and retrieval.

Link the new material to what you already know

As understanding depends on linking your ideas together, ask yourself, 'What does this remind me of?' whenever you come across a new concept in your subject. Try to summarise 2–3 main ideas or learning points from the material in question and link them with what you already know. These tips are based on the principle of elaborative rehearsal that applies to storage and retrieval processes in memory (and which I explained earlier in the section on 'working memory'). Remember: *asking questions* before you study is an elaborative learning strategy.

Pause and check that you understand what you've read

In general, people's understanding of what they have read improves significantly when they pause to check what they have learned. This activity is called 'comprehension monitoring' and it enriches your storage and retrieval processes. It involves asking yourself such questions as: *Do I understand the main idea in this passage? Does it make sense to me? How can I explain it in my own words?*

Test yourself regularly: The retrieval practice effect

For over a century, it has been known that testing yourself regularly to see if you can retrieve what you've learned improves your long-term memory (Abbott, 1909). This phenomenon is called the 'testing effect' or the 'retrieval practice effect' (Bjork et al., 2013) and suggests that, when you're preparing for a test, practising the retrieval of information from your memory is more effective than merely re-reading the material that you've been studying (Roediger & Kapicke, 2006). But learning in university is *shared* as well as solitary, and digital platforms like VLEs offer exciting opportunities for you to test your knowledge by interacting with, and questioning, other learners in your modules (see Chapter 4).

Form a study group to share and discuss the material

Collaborating with your classmates in small study groups is a good way of challenging your understanding of a given topic. Here are some tips to optimise the work done in your study group:

- Agree on a set of clear ground rules for the specific objectives of your study group and for your duties and responsibilities as members. Otherwise, the group could become a disorganised 'talking shop'.

- Agree in advance what the group should do if one of the members fails to deliver material as promised or otherwise breaks the rules of the group.

- The group should be small enough to facilitate discussion – perhaps comprising no more than 4–5 students.

- If possible, meet at the same time and in the same place each week for no more than an hour.

- Try to meet in an environment that is quiet and conducive to learning such as a study room in the library – not in refectories, bars or in open-air settings where distractions are pervasive.

- Make sure that every member of a study group participates actively. One way of achieving this goal is to elect a chairperson who assigns specific topics to each member of the group. This role of chairperson should rotate around all members.

- The chairperson bears responsibility for assigning topics, encouraging contributions from all members, ensuring that everyone gets an opportunity to speak at the meetings and timing the proceedings.

- Avoid sharing writing tasks among group members. This practice could lead to copying and pasting material that you have not written into your essays and whose sources may be unknown – a process that could lead to unintentional plagiarism (see also Chapter 9).

PRACTICAL STRATEGIES TO IMPROVE ROTE LEARNING

In the previous section, I explained how to improve 'meaningful learning', or your ability to understand things. But, occasionally, you will have to memorize information through repetition without any need for understanding because this information provides the building blocks for mastering more complex ideas. One example of this is in learning anatomical terminology. What are the names of the cranial nerves? Or what are the main parts of the ear? In both cases, some degree of rote learning is required before you can move on to tackling deeper issues concerning how these systems work.

In order to master rote learning tasks, **mnemonics** like rhymes and acronyms are particularly useful. To illustrate, a rhyme like 'On Old Olympia's Towering Top A Finn And German Viewed Some Hops' may help you to remember the names of the 12 cranial nerves (olfactory, optic, oculomotor, trochlear, trigeminal, abducens, facial, auditory, glossopharyngeal, vagus, sensory (accessory) and hypoglossal; Herlevich, 1990). Similarly, the acronym PET can be used to recall the names of the different parts of the ear – pinna, ear canal and tympanic membrane. In Box 8.4, I present a list of mnemonics that can help you to learn things off by heart.

Box 8.4 Techniques for improving rote learning

Mnemonic	Description	Example
Method of *Loci*: walking through your mind palace	Imagine placing each item that you want to remember in a particular place in a familiar setting such as a room in your house.	In medicine, you could learn a recommended sequence of antiarrhythmic drugs by 'placing' them in different locations along a familiar route in your home (e.g. from your kitchen to the front door).
Keyword method of foreign vocabulary learning	Form a link between a new word or term in a foreign language and a familiar one in your native language (but beware of 'false friends' that appear similar to each other but have different meanings).	In Spanish, the word for 'cow' is 'vaca' – imagine a cow with a vacuum cleaner in a field.
Acrostics	Devise a sentence in which the first letters of each word represent the items to be remembered.	In music, the sentence 'Every Good Boy Deserves Fruit' (E, G, B, D, F) will help you to remember the names of the notes on the treble clef.
Acronyms	Devise a word whose letters stand for the items to be remembered.	In psychology, 'SMART' summarises the features needed for maximum motivation: the goals should be specific, measurable, action-related, realistic and time-based (see also Box 2.4, p. 24).

Let's explore two of these memory techniques in more detail – the Method of Loci and the keyword method.

The Method of *Loci*

The Method of *Loci* (MOL or the 'mind palace' mnemonic) is a useful technique for remembering a list or sequence of information. Used by Sherlock Holmes in the television series *Sherlock* (Zielinski, 2014), it involves creating a mental image to associate the items to be remembered with specific locations in a familiar environment. This technique dates back to the Greek poet Simonides of Ceos from the fifth century B. C. According to legend, he was the sole survivor of a tragic banquet hall collapse and was asked to give an account of who had been buried in the debris. Remarkably, by visualizing where each guest had been sitting at the banquet table (a familiar environment), he could accurately recall the identity of each victim of the accident. Subsequently, he proposed that a good way to remember a sequence of things is by constructing a location in your imagination (a mind palace) and by filling it with mental images of the things that need to be recalled. When you're finished, you can walk through your mind palace at any time in the future to recall any item in its correct place in the sequence.

MOL is effective for two reasons. By laying out unrelated items of information as signposts on a familiar route, the MOL exploits the navigational skills in which we excel as a species. By associating the items to be remembered with locations on a familiar route, it binds the memory trace for these items into a bigger assembly of brain cells than if you had tried to learn them one by one. Interestingly, Joshua Foer used the MOL when he competed in the USA Memory Championships in 2006 (Foer, 2011). One of the tasks in this competition required him to memorise the order of two shuffled decks of playing cards. By imagining these cards placed in various locations in his house, Foer was able to correctly remember the order of the cards in the two decks in under 2 minutes! In university, research shows that the MOL can be used to improve the learning of technical information in macro-economics (Shaughnessy & White, 2012) and endocrinology (Qureshi et al., 2014).

The keyword method

The keyword method of foreign vocabulary learning involves forming a mental image of a word in your native language which in some way resembles a foreign language word that you wish to learn (Gruneberg, 1987). To illustrate this method in action, consider a well-known study by Raugh & Atkinson (1975). These researchers compared two ways of learning Spanish words. The first method involved traditional rote learning, or trying to memorise English translations of Spanish words off-by-heart. The second technique involved the keyword method whereby students were taught to *add meaning* to their learning in two stages. They were encouraged to think of an English word that sounded like the Spanish word in question (e.g. charcoal for the Spanish word *charco*, meaning 'puddle'). This English word served as a keyword. Then, they had to form an *interactive mental image* of this keyword embedded in its actual English translation: imagine a block of charcoal lying in a puddle. Results showed that students using the keyword method recalled an average of 88 per cent of the Spanish vocabulary words. Those in the rote-learning group could recall only 28 per cent of these words. Further support for the keyword method was provided by Gruneberg & Jacobs (1991) who discovered that it helped a group of executives to learn about 400 Spanish words and some basic grammar in only 12 hours of teaching. This method, however, must come with a warning for 'false friends', where learners make common errors in translating one word for a similar-sounding word in their own language. For example, 'J'assiste à un concert' means 'I go to a concert' in French, not 'I assist at a concert'. It is important to keep keywords separate from translations in order to use this mnemonic correctly.

Before we conclude this section, I will explain why the mnemonics listed in Box 8.4 and Box 8.5 help to improve your memory. They work by strengthening each of the three stages of memory I outlined earlier in this chapter, and they encourage you to pay more attention to the material to be learned initially, thereby enhancing the encoding process. Mnemonics facilitate the meaningful organisation (or 'chunking') of the material. They also improve the retrieval process by training you to associate new information with familiar cues. But the paradox of mnemonics is that they don't actually simplify what you have to learn – instead, they *elaborate* upon it. Therefore, they allow you to store *more* rather than less knowledge about the material in question. This reminds us of a principle that we encountered earlier in this chapter: the more you know, the more you can remember.

TEN PRINCIPLES OF REMEMBERING AND UNDERSTANDING

Here is a summary of ten key principles of understanding and memory that you encountered in this chapter:

1. Organisation: Chunking improves your recall of material
Organising individual items into meaningful groups (or chunks) helps to improve the span of your working memory.

2. Construction: We build our memories
Remembering is a constructive process in which we use prior knowledge and expectations to build an interpretation of what happened in the past.

3. Overlearning: Review what you have learned one more time
Your memory can be improved by developing the habit of reviewing what you learned at the end of a study session – even if you feel sure that you have mastered the material adequately.

4. Depth of processing: The importance of asking questions
The durability of your memories is influenced by the depth of questioning (or level of processing) that you initially conducted on the material. The deepest level of processing involves asking questions about what the material means and how it relates to what you already know.

5. Maintenance rehearsal: Rote learning
Information can be kept alive in your working memory by repeating it to yourself (rote repetition). Unfortunately, as soon as you stop the practise of repeating the information, it will disappear.

6. Elaborative rehearsal: Making connections deepens your understanding

Elaborative rehearsal involves thinking about what the to-be-remembered material means and how it is related to what you already know.

7. Schemas: Headings can improve your understanding

Looking for an appropriate heading or schema at the encoding stage improves your understanding and memory of the material to be learned.

8. Knowledge-based effect: The more you know, the more you will remember in that area

The more you know about a specific field (the larger your 'knowledge-base'), the better will be your memory for new information in that field because you can connect it to the 'scaffolding' of relevant existing knowledge.

9. State-dependency: The encoding-specificity principle of memory

You are more likely to remember information (retrieval process) under the same conditions in which you learned it. This principle applies both to physical environments (the 'context-dependency' of learning) and to psychological environments (the 'state-dependency' of learning).

10. Retrieval practice: The testing effect

Testing yourself regularly to see if you can remember what you've learned improves your long-term memory. Revision works best if it involves frequent testing of what you can remember rather than merely re-reading the material that you have studied.

SUMMARY

The purpose of this chapter was to provide some scientific principles and practical tips on how to improve your ability to remember and understand new information. In the introduction, I distinguished between two types of learning tasks: those that involve 'meaningful learning' and those that involve 'rote learning'. Meaningful learning requires abstract thinking in which you try to understand new concepts and ideas and apply them successfully to challenging tasks (e.g. writing a research assignment). By contrast, rote learning involves memorising facts such as the periodic table in chemistry or foreign vocabulary in language studies. In university, the vast majority of your learning falls into the 'meaningful' category because it's motivated by a clear and specific purpose: to improve your knowledge and skills in the subjects that you have chosen to study).

The chapter was organised into sections as follows:

- I explored the nature, stages and stores of your memory system. Here, I explained the three stages of memory as encoding, storage and retrieval.

- I then described three memory stores: sensory memory, working memory and long-term memory.

- I provided seven practical strategies for improving your ability to understand new material. These strategies included:

  1 Asking questions (the PQRR technique)
  2 Paying more attention to what you learn
  3 Using headings to organise the information to be learned
  4 Linking new material with what you already know
  5 Pausing frequently to check that you understand what you're reading
  6 Testing yourself regularly
  7 Discussing the material in study groups.

- I gave you practical tips on some mnemonics (memory aids) to improve rote learning (repeating things off by heart). Here, I focused on the Method of *Loci* and the keyword technique.

- The final section of the chapter summarised ten scientific principles of remembering and understanding.

Answer to memory puzzle in Box 8.1

The 24 digits are generated by the rule 'square the numbers from 1 to 12'. Thus the square of 1 is 1, the square of 2 is 4 and so on, until the last number, 144, which is the square of 12.

THE LAST THING ONE FINDS OUT WHEN CONSTRUCTING A WORK IS WHAT TO PUT FIRST.

Blaise Pascal (1670)

with contributions from Helen O'Shea

Chapter 9

Managing Research Assignments
Projects, Talks and Poster Presentations

INTRODUCTION

The skills of marshalling relevant evidence, drawing valid conclusions and expressing them clearly and concisely have long been admired as distinctive characteristics of the educated mind. Surveys of employers reveal that thinking and communication skills are highly valued in graduate job seekers (Higher Education Authority, 2015). Similarly, interviews for academic posts in universities typically require candidates to give an oral presentation or 'job talk'. Because of this, you will be expected to complete various research assignments in university such as essays, term papers, project dissertations and oral and poster presentations that are intended to evaluate and improve your writing and presentation skills. In general, these assignments have three main objectives:

- They assess the degree to which you can apply general academic knowledge to address specific questions and problems

- They train you to master certain writing and presentation conventions in your discipline. You will learn how and when to cite evidence in support of your arguments and how to present your academic work effectively to an audience

- Research assignments help you to clarify and make explicit your thinking about a given topic.

To help you to manage these tasks successfully, the purpose of the present chapter is to provide some practical advice on planning, researching, writing and presenting your academic assignments.

This chapter is organised as follows:

....

➤ I'll consider the problem of planning an essay or paper assignment.

➤ I'll present some practical guidelines on how to research it as thoroughly as possible.

➤ I'll explore some strategies for writing a first draft of your work.

➤ I'll explain how rewriting is the key to producing a final draft of your assignment.

➤ I'll give you some practical tips on creating and delivering effective presentations – including both oral (talks) and poster presentations.

....

PLANNING: CLARIFYING YOUR RESEARCH QUESTIONS

Research is difficult because nobody tells you how to start or when to stop writing. To overcome this problem, you need to do three things:

• Clarify the requirements of your assignment

• Choose your research topic and

• Outline your specific research question(s).

Clarify the requirements of your assignment

The first step in conducting a research assignment is to find out exactly what's expected of you. For this task, don't rely on second-hand information, which is invariably incomplete or inaccurate. The best way to establish the requirements of your assignment is to read the details given to you online or on hand-outs and then to ask questions of the academic staff if you are unclear about anything (see Box 9.1).

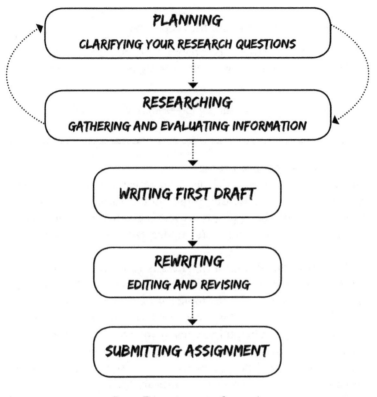

Fig 9.1: The main stages of research

Box 9.1 Clarifying your assignment: Some questions to ask your department or school

---

Here are some questions to ask the professors who are responsible for your assignment.

1 If an academic supervisor is required, will you be assigned one by the department or school or do you have to find one yourself?

2 Where can you read and download the regulations that apply to your research assignment?

3 What exactly are you expected to deliver in this assignment (e.g. word length, structure and content of the material)?

4 What is the deadline for submission of the assignment? Does it require an electronic and/or hard-copy submission?

5 What system of stylistic conventions is required for your assignment? This could include margin width, spacing or reference citation and footnote style.

6 Is it possible to read or see a good example of the type of assignment that is required of you?

Choose your research topic

The next step in the initial phase of research is to choose your research topic. Ideally, this topic should satisfy at least three criteria: it should be appropriate, feasible and appealing to you – but not necessarily original (at undergraduate level, you're still 'learning the ropes').

The criterion of appropriateness is satisfied if your topic is approved formally by your department or school. Of course, this problem does not arise if the topic has been assigned to you but it could become an issue if you have to devise the topic yourself. In this latter case, it is helpful to consult your professors for possible project ideas. The advantage of this approach is that it ensures that your supervisor will be interested in your work. Other strategies for generating possible research topics are listed in Box 9.2.

The second criterion for a suitable research topic is that it should be feasible or manageable within the time limit and resources available to you. For example, it wouldn't be advisable to undertake an assignment on a topic for which there are few or no library resources. In general, the most feasible research topics are those that have generated sufficient research literature to whet your appetite but not so much as to overwhelm you with technical detail.

Thirdly, the topic for your assignment should hold some interest for you as you will be studying it for some time. But what makes a topic interesting? Remember from Chapter 6 that studying requires a decision to invest mental effort in what you're doing. Don't wait for something to interest you – take the initiative by asking as many questions as possible about it. The clearer and more specific your questions, the greater their power to focus your interest.

Box 9.2 Generating ideas for possible research topics

Here are some practical tips to help you to generate suitable research questions. Always check your ideas with your formal supervisor.

- Ask your professors for information about research projects that they are currently working on so that your work may be of assistance to them.

- Look at projects by previous students and try to modify or extend one of them.

- Find an exam question from a previous year and try to re-formulate it as a research question for your project.

- Keep an 'idea file' of research suggestions/new directions that you come across in your reading of recent studies.

- Skim through the contents pages of a major journal in your field, paying special attention to the suggestions for further research in the discussion section.

Outline your specific research question(s)

The next stage in the research process is to specify as precisely as possible the question(s) that you wish to answer. Remember that statements are not questions. If your friend tells you that she is studying early twentieth-century Irish poets, then you have a description of her topic. However, if she says 'I'm trying to find out what influence the 1916 Rising had on the themes of Irish poets in the 1920s,' then you can identify her research question and become more involved in her work. This example shows that questions generate more interest than do statements.

Not surprisingly, successful researchers understand this difference between a topic and a question. A topic may refer to a general academic field (e.g. law of contract), but a research question is a specific problem within that area (e.g. 'What constitutes 'economic duress' in contract?'). A list of sample research questions is presented in Box 5.4, Chapter 5.

When you have specified your research question as precisely as possible, it's essential to calculate how much time you will have for your project (see also Chapter 3). A useful tip here is to *work backwards* from the date of submission to the present time. Remember, *everything takes longer* than you expect when conducting research! To counteract this problem, and to apply the SMART approach described in Chapter 2, give yourself a specific starting and finishing time for each step of your proposed research plan.

RESEARCHING: GATHERING AND EVALUATING RELEVANT INFORMATION

The next major stage of research is to gather and evaluate relevant information. This data-gathering work involves at least four key tasks.

- Locating relevant background literature
- Evaluating the information you find
- Taking useful notes
- Documenting your reference sources correctly.

Locating relevant background literature

The amount of background research you conduct for your assignment will depend on such factors as the nature and length of your assignment (e.g. is it a weekly legal case-study or a year-long dissertation?), its importance (e.g. what proportion of end-of-year marks does it count for?) and the subject matter involved (e.g. whether it is library- or laboratory-based). At this stage, it's essential to learn how to use to all the electronic resources and databases that are available through your university library in your subject. If possible, keep a written statement of your research question to hand when you start your literature search. This statement should contain key words that will guide your search.

Evaluating the information you find

Locating relevant research literature only tells you what other people have done. It does not tell you how valid this information is or what to do next. Therefore, the next stage of research is to conduct a literature review or critical evaluation of relevant information. Practical tips on critical evaluation are provided in Chapter 7.

Taking useful notes

As you use your critical reading checklist, make summary notes that are relevant to your specific research question(s) (see advice on note-taking in Chapter 5). Otherwise, you may end up with a series of unrelated facts from different studies. Unfortunately, there is nothing more dreary to read than an essay or paper that comprises a funeral parade of unrelated facts.

Documenting your reference sources correctly

Develop the habit of recording the complete publication details of any reference sources, such as books and articles, that you intend to use in your assignment. A number of reference management and citation management systems are available commercially to organise the citations and documents that you gather through your literature searches. Popular options in this regard are systems such as Mendeley, EndNote, RefWorks and Wikindx. Most such systems enable you to insert citations in your text, create a reference list (bibliography) to appear at the end of your essay or paper and to match citations with your listed references. Some systems such as Mendeley also contain networking features that allow you share citations and documents with other students, thereby facilitating collaborative group projects or group presentations. Regardless of the system that you use, however, be careful to record the exact page numbers of any direct quotations that you plan to include in your assignment. If you fail to acknowledge these details in your citations, you may be guilty of using other people's material as your own – a serious offence called '**plagiarism**'. This term refers to the inclusion of another person's writing or ideas in any formally presented work that form part of the requirements of a module without due acknowledgement or citation of the original source of the material (University College Dublin, 2005). Put simply, plagiarism involves copying other people's writing, work or ideas and subsequently passing them off as your own material in your essays, papers, projects, lab reports, and oral or poster presentations. Make sure to check your university's policy on this egregious misconduct.

WRITING THE FIRST DRAFT

Having located and evaluated relevant literature, you should now begin to write a first draft of your assignment. The purpose of this draft is to clarify your own thinking about the project. The second draft will address the task of communicating this information clearly to the reader. Before you begin, you should become familiar with the stages of writing a first draft.

- Planning your work

- Making a preliminary outline of your essay or paper

- Organising your ideas

- Writing the introduction to the assignment: Do it last

- Working on the main body of the text

- Identifying and explaining your conclusions

- Writing a summary of your work

- The format and presentation of your work.

Planning your work

Your work should adhere to the following four criteria:

Your work should be well-written

Your writing must be clear and coherent. This requirement stems from the fact that, unless you are examined orally, your reader will not be able to question you directly about what you have written.

Unless you are very lucky or extremely gifted, you will not be able to write an adequate essay or report in one sitting. Therefore, all you should concern yourself with at this stage is to get your ideas down on paper in any order. You can reorganise them later. That is why, to paraphrase Nabokov (see Chapter 5), good writing depends on substantial rewriting, or the art of refining your ideas progressively.

In addition, when you write, you must be punctilious about citing appropriate reference sources for any ideas or quotations that you have borrowed from other authors, otherwise you may be charged with plagiarism.

Finally, you should realise that considerable effort is required to write an assignment clearly and with an appealing flow. In other words, good writing depends more on perspiration than on inspiration. What makes any piece of writing clear and persuasive? At least three criteria spring to mind, which are addressed in the next three sections.

Your work should answer the question asked

All too often, students re-interpret an essay title to mean 'Write whatever comes to mind about X'. By taking this approach, you are ignoring the specific question or issue raised by the title of the essay and are in danger of going off on an irrelevant tangent. Always keep the essay title in mind when structuring your work.

Your work should draw on relevant supporting evidence

Most written assignments in university require you to look up appropriate course material before you answer the specific question under investigation. Writing allows you to use relevant course work as evidence to support what you wish to say.

Your work should present a coherent argument or story

The evidence and arguments in a well-written assignment need to hang together coherently. There are three main strategies for achieving this coherence.

1   Proper planning and clear, structured organisation. You should allocate a separate paragraph to each main idea.

2   The use of 'signpost words' such as 'therefore', 'thus' or 'however'.

3   The discipline of engaging in successive revisions of your work.

Making a preliminary outline of your essay or paper

Before you begin to write, make a roadmap or outline of the sequence of your ideas. This outline should address such issues as your specific research question(s), the scope and limitations of your assignment and the evidence and arguments that you wish to cite in support of them. If you find it difficult to specify your research questions clearly, then you need to go back to the drawing board and analyse the topic of the assignment once more.

In general, a good outline should examine both the content and structure of your assignment. With regard to content, what is the main conclusion, point or argument that you wish to present? What would you like readers to believe or to do after they have read your work? What evidence, arguments or examples can you use to support your position? Turning to structural issues, you should ask yourself the following questions: what are the main ideas that serve as a foundation for your assignment, and what is the optimum sequence in which to present these ideas so that they flow logically?

Unless your assignment has a pre-determined format, as is found in laboratory reports in psychology, you will have to design the scaffolding or structure of your work on your own. In this regard, it may help to divide the assignment into three parts: beginning (introduction), middle (main body) and end (conclusions and implications). The purpose of the introduction is to explain the background to your research question(s). The main body of the report conveys details of relevant evidence and arguments. The conclusion draws together your argument or findings in a concise manner. It is important to note, however, that the first draft of the introduction, main body and conclusions of your assignment do not have to be written in the sequence in which they are presented.

Having created an outline of your paper, the next job is to rearrange your notes in the appropriate sequence. Then, give yourself an uninterrupted period of time (e.g. 1–2 hours) and start writing. As this is the first draft, your main objective at this stage should be to get all your ideas down on paper. Once the essential details are in place, you can revise the paper at your leisure.

Organising your ideas

Having sketched an outline of the content and structure of your assignment, the next task is to impose some kind of organisation on your ideas. This involves making decisions about which points and which lines of evidence 'hang together' and, also, how they can be arranged in a coherent sequence or narrative.

In general, each of your key points should be given a separate paragraph. One suggestion is to begin each paragraph either with a topic sentence (a general statement about the issue being discussed) or with a transition word or phrase (see Box 9.3 for some examples). The remaining sentences in the paragraph should explain, expand, illustrate or modify this central point. Usually, it is best to present the topic sentence first so that the reader will have some idea of what to expect in the paragraph. In other words, the first sentence of every paragraph should act as an 'advance organiser' for the remaining material in it.

Writing the introduction to the assignment: Do it last

The purpose of the introduction is to set the scene for your assignment. As a first step in this task, you need to specify the scope and limitations, or boundaries, that you have chosen for your work. By outlining what you intend to cover and by indicating what you intend to omit, you are indirectly specifying the criteria by which you wish your assignment to be judged

Experienced researchers tend to write the introduction last. Recall what the French philosopher Pascal said about this strategy at the beginning of this chapter: the last thing one finds out when constructing a work is what to put first. This advice may surprise you, but there are several reasons for this strategy.

- It will give your writing an attractive flow because, by knowing what your conclusions are, you can introduce enough background material to ensure that there is a visible narrative thread linking the material together.

- Leaving the introduction until the end reduces the likelihood of including irrelevant material in the introduction.

- When you know what your conclusions are, you will be in a good position to devise an imaginative or engaging opening to your work.

This advice is particularly relevant to essays and papers in Arts and Humanities subjects like English, history or philosophy where a good paper presents a theme or argument in the opening paragraph rather than merely summarising a range of isolated facts (e.g. the relevance of a specific author, idea or theory to a current issue in the field). If you're not sure how to do this, ask your professors or tutors to refer you to examples of well-crafted, scholarly and accessible articles in your academic discipline. Reading seminal essays can help you to develop your own writing style. The golden rule is to provide the reader with only enough information to enable her or him to understand the background to, and significance of, your specific question. Don't include excessive or irrelevant historical details.

Working on the main body of the text

Start with the middle part or main body of the assignment. Your task here is to ensure that you cover what you said you would include (refer to the 'scope and limitations' section in your introduction). The key issue at this stage is whether or not you have made sufficient points to support your conclusions. You must substantiate all your claims with appropriate evidence. Therefore, you must learn the art of referring to, or quoting from, scholarly sources in an effort to buttress your argument or exposition. Don't worry if the structure of your report changes as you make progress in writing the main body of the paper. It's quite common for writers to discover that the expression of one idea triggers another idea that challenges assumptions in the introduction.

Identifying and explaining your conclusions

The final section of your assignment contains your conclusions. Here, your task is to indicate what follows from your central arguments or to state your conclusions explicitly. Ideally, your conclusions should be numbered or organised in such a way as to provide a general answer to your initial research question. As well as being cautious about premature extrapolation from your conclusions, you should outline some specific suggestions for future research on the topic you have addressed.

Writing a summary of your work

Many undergraduate assignments (e.g. project reports in the sciences and social sciences) require an abstract or brief summary of your work to be included on a separate page, usually amounting to no more than 200 words. This abstract should be presented immediately after the title page and before the introduction. The purpose of the abstract is to explain concisely what research question you tackled, what evidence or arguments you presented and what conclusions you drew.

The format and presentation of your work

The publication conventions surrounding academic assignments, such as how to cite and present references, vary from subject to subject. You must familiarise yourself thoroughly with the writing and stylistic conventions of your discipline. This information should be available from academic staff.

REWRITING: EDITING AND REVISING

Successful writing looks easy – but it isn't. Good writing involves rewriting: it depends on a careful and systematic refinement of your preliminary drafts. How can you get from a disjointed initial draft to a polished and persuasive final version?

The initial step in this process of revision involves reading your first draft from start to finish. Then read this draft again – but this time, more slowly and more critically. Make annotations and amendments to the text as you go along. You should pay attention to at least four issues:

- Coverage
- Coherence
- Presentation
- Review.

Coverage: Did you fulfil your stated objectives?

An important criterion to use when evaluating your first draft concerns the issue of whether or not you have adequately covered everything that you said you would include. In other words, does the content reflect your intent as stated in the scope and limitations part of your introduction? When this question is posed, most people discover that some of their best points are not explained clearly enough or are missing. Although this discovery is disappointing, it is better for you to discover the gaps in your work at this stage rather than at a later date. By the way, you may find it helpful to ask a second reader, such as one of your classmates, to comment briefly on the content and layout of your assignment.

Coherence: Do your ideas hang together?

The next criterion of effective writing concerns the coherence of the assignment. Do your ideas fit together neatly or do they appear to be random and disjointed? If there is neither a coherence nor a flow to your ideas, then you should consider using one or more of the following techniques.

Check that your headings and subheadings are accurate and in the correct place. If the organisation of the paper is unclear or idiosyncratic, then the reader will not know what to expect next and her or his surprise will soon turn to exasperation.

You should develop a skill in using 'transition words' to achieve a seamless connection between your paragraphs. These words provide the cement between the building blocks of your ideas. Some of them are listed in Box 9.3.

For optimal flow in a paper, try to ensure that your conclusions are clearly apparent to the reader. A good way to do this is to write in your introduction: 'In this paper, I shall argue that . . .'. If your conclusions aren't easy to locate or understand, your work will appear to be confusing and incomplete.

Presentation: Does your assignment look professional?

The more professional the appearance of your assignment, the more marks it will attract. When checking your first draft, you should assess the clarity, grammar and style of your work.

Clarity

The clarity of an assignment can be assessed only with the assistance of another reader. For example, you could ask a classmate or a friend to check that she or he understands what you have written – a favour that you can reciprocate by reading her or his project. This second reading is helpful because writers tend to become so familiar with their own work that they find it difficult to assess it objectively.

Grammar

You should check that your spelling and grammar are satisfactory. Given the ubiquity of computerised spelling checkers, there is no excuse for errors in this aspect of your work. Also, you should use the active rather than the passive voice whenever possible. This advice is based on the theory that statements written in the passive voice tend to be duller and more difficult to read than those expressed in the active voice. For example, 'Michael Collins said that . . .' is more vibrant than 'It was once said by Michael Collins that . . .' .

Style
You should check that you have complied fully with the stylistic conventions of your assignment. For example, when citing references using your recommended house style, you will need to check whether it is conventional to use endnotes, or to include the author's surname and year of publication in line. Although these conventions vary considerably from subject to subject, it is your responsibility to learn the stylistic requirements of your subject. Footnotes are commonly used in the Arts and Humanities (e.g. philosophy and English), but they are quite rare in the social sciences. In view of such stylistic variation, make sure to check a publication manual in your subject or else request written guidelines from your department before you begin your final draft. Avoid the use of sexist language also (e.g. 'she or he' is more appropriate than 'he' when talking about people in general).

Review: Does your assignment satisfy requirements?
Having rewritten your assignment, you should review it once more using the following checklist:

1   What is your research question?

2   Are you sure that you have addressed all of the key words in the title of the assignment?

3   Did you cover what you said you would cover?

4   Does the paper or essay satisfy all relevant academic departmental regulations with regard to format and word length?

5   Does your work have a clear beginning and end? Is the layout and paragraph structure acceptable?

6   Are all tables, graphs and other figures readily comprehensible and clearly labelled?

7 Have you listed precise references for each name that you cite in your assignment? If so, are your references accurate and presented correctly?

8 Does the paper flow smoothly? If not, try inserting transition words and phrases at the junctions between paragraphs (see Box 9.3).

Box 9.3 Some useful transition words and phrases

One of the key skills of effective writing is to ensure that ideas flow smoothly between paragraphs. This fluency is best achieved by using transition words. These words are linking devices or linguistic signposts that provide good clues to the organisation of the material as well as indicating that something important is about to be presented. Here are some examples (from Deem, 1993; Marshall & Rowland, 1993).

Transition word or phrase	Function in writing
For example; for instance; to illustrate	To signal examples
Further; furthermore; in addition; also; in addition; moreover; next	To provide extra information
Likewise; similarly; also	To indicate a comparison
But; nevertheless; in contrast; on the other hand; conversely	To indicate a contrast
Therefore; overall; accordingly; so; consequently; thus	To indicate a cause-and-effect or a result or conclusion
First; second; third; finally; later; next; in the meantime; meanwhile	To indicate a chronological organisation or connection in time
In conclusion; to conclude; in other words; in short; on the whole	To provide a summary

---

SUBMITTING THE ASSIGNMENT

When you're happy with the final draft of the assignment, you should proofread it very carefully. Print out your assignment a day or two before the submission deadline to avoid any last-minute problems with computers. Get a receipt from your academic department or school when you submit the assignment formally. Don't resort to shoving your submission under the door of a professor on the evening of the deadline.

RESPONDING TO FEEDBACK ON YOUR ASSIGNMENT

The process of writing an academic assignment is cyclical. It involves processes like planning, drafting, revising and rewriting various drafts of your material. You might think that this cycle culminates in the submission of your work, but you would be wrong – there's another step in the research process. This step involves using feedback on, and constructive criticism of, what you've written to improve the quality of your work. Here are some practical tips on how best to respond to comments and feedback from your tutors, supervisors or professors.

- Try not to take the comments or feedback personally – they're intended to *improve* your work, not to criticise you. All they show is that your work isn't as good as it can be at present.

- When reading your professors' feedback, it's helpful to distinguish between 'higher order' (content) and 'lower order' (format) comments. Typically, higher order issues determine the quality of your grade – although lower order issues are important too.

- Higher order comments concern 'big picture' details of the substance and structure of your work. For example, does your paper or essay show evidence of a deep and broad knowledge of the topic and of extensive reading or evaluation of relevant research? Does it have a coherent message, angle or argument? Is it supported by appropriate evidence? Does it show evidence of original insights and of critical thinking? Is it logically organised and written clearly, accurately and concisely?

- Lower order comments concern the grammar, style and formatting issues of your work.

- When feedback on your writing is negative, it's easy to lose heart, but effective writing requires perseverance. As Dorothy Parker allegedly remarked, 'I hate writing but I love having written.' Encouragingly, many of the world's most successful writers persisted in the face of repeated rejection. For example, J. K. Rowling's first Harry Potter manuscript, *Harry Potter and the Philosopher's Stone*, was turned down by 12 different publishers before it was accepted by Bloomsbury (Runcie, 2016). Her books have now sold hundreds of millions of copies.

PRACTICAL TIPS ON EFFECTIVE ORAL PRESENTATIONS AND TALKS

Giving an academic talk in the form of a lecture or research seminar to an audience that includes classmates, other students and your professors can be a daunting experience.

- You may be shy and try to avoid being the focus of other people's attention where possible.

- You may fear the possibility of being evaluated negatively by your listeners or of being unable to answer their questions afterwards.

- Simply due to a lack of practice, you may have very little confidence in your ability to give a talk to others.

For such reasons, at least 25 per cent of people dread the prospect of having to speak in public (Tsaousides, 2017). Take heart: with proper preparation and plenty of practice, you can become highly skilled at telling the story of your work. Intriguingly, research shows that the human brain is hardwired for making connections through storytelling (Bhalia, 2013) – so your audience is *biologically disposed* to be interested in what you have to say.

According to Kosslyn (2011), to be effective, your presentation must satisfy three criteria.

- Just like any good story, it should make a connection with the audience.

- It must focus the audience's attention on what is most relevant in your talk – your key message.

- It should lead members of the audience to understand and remember what you say.

With these ideas in mind, here are some practical tips on delivering effective oral presentations (see also Dolan, 2017; Kosslyn, 2011; Lightheart, 2016; Northey & Timney, 2015). These tips concern three key steps: preparing your presentation, giving your talk and answering questions from the audience.

Step 1: Preparing your presentation

Preparing a presentation involves knowing your audience, planning your presentation, preparing your slides, considering your conclusions and rehearsing your talk.

Know your audience

Who are you speaking to and how much do you think they know about your topic? The answer to this question should help you to pitch your talk at the right level. Is your audience a specialist group with roughly the same knowledge of your topic as you have? Or a general audience of people who are interested in your field but know very little about your topic? Will it be a mixed audience combining people with specialist knowledge and general interest? Knowing your audience will help you to calibrate the level of your talk appropriately.

Plan your presentation

According to Kosslyn (2011), an effective presentation is like a pair of bookends on either side of a set of books. The first bookend is the introduction, the books themselves are the main body of your talk and the second bookend is the conclusion or wrap-up. Interestingly, when we're presented with a sequence of information, we remember best what came first ('**primacy effect**') and what came last ('**recency effect**') but we find it difficult to recall the details in the middle. The practical implication of this finding is that the beginning and end of your presentation should convey the main message that you'd like your audience to remember. Here's a practical checklist to consider for each of the three sections of your talk.

Beginning (introduction)

- Introduce yourself on the title slide (name, affiliation and email address, if relevant).

- State your objectives clearly in the second slide.

- Give a quick overview or roadmap of your presentation in the third slide and state your key message.

- If possible, provide a verbal opening 'hook' (a relevant quote, question or anecdote) both to capture the interest of your audience and to convey the theme or message of your talk.

Middle (body of your presentation)

- If you're reporting the results of an empirical study, tell the story of your work by explaining what you did, how you did it and what you discovered, and acknowledge any limitations of your study.

- If your talk is not empirically based, explain your main ideas with supporting evidence in a logical sequence before reaching your conclusions.

- Have you provided enough concrete evidence and examples to support your argument(s)? Is the level of detail of your points appropriate to your audience?

- Have you considered using any active learning techniques such as exercises or demonstrations of what you're talking about to increase audience attention?

End (wrap-up or 'take home' message)

- What do you want your audience to understand or be able to do as a result of your talk? State your main 'take home' message or conclusion(s) in relation to your objectives: a good way to do this is to present a modified version of your 'objectives' slide to update the audience on what you'd like them to remember.

- If the members of your audience were asked to summarise your 'take home' message in 1–2 sentences, what would they say? Use the 'take home' message slide to signal the end of your talk explicitly ('This concludes my talk') – don't fade out aimlessly ('I think that's enough from me').

- Decide whether to give a handout to your audience members or to refer them to the URL of your website. Kosslyn (2011) recommends the latter option because encouraging people to visit your website exposes them to more information about your work than you could fit in a handout.

Prepare your slides
- Use a simple slide template design: don't distract the audience with quirky and unnecessary pictures or graphics. Use simple transitions.

- Be careful when using video clips embedded in your slide presentation – they don't always run smoothly on different types of laptop and are notoriously memory-intensive.

- Use as many slides as you need in order to ensure that your presentation is clear and compelling: as a general rule, try to use one slide for every one minute of your talk. If all the text you want to include doesn't fit on a single slide, allow it to run over to a new slide.

- Use a plain font such as Arial, Calibri or another well-known sans serif font. Choose an appropriate font size (28 to 32 points).

- Organise the information in your slides using evidence-based guidelines (e.g. see Box 9.4).

As you become a more confident presenter, you'll find that you need fewer slides – but ones that are better calibrated to your audience's needs and expectations.

Box 9.4 How to organise information in slides

Here are six of Kosslyn's (2011) 'cognitive communication rules' for organising information in your slides.

Name of rule	Meaning of rule	Practical tip
'Goldilocks' rule	Include just the right amount of information.	Present the amount of detail that is appropriate for the point that you're making – no more and no less.
'Birds of a feather' rule	Information that's grouped together is easier for us understand than information presented separately.	Group similar information to make it easy to understand and remember.
Rule of four	We find it difficult to take in more than four ideas or points at a time.	Present four or fewer bullet points per main point.
'Rudolph the red-nosed reindeer' rule	We pay attention to anything that looks different or stands out.	Your most important information must look more important than anything else.
'Mr Magoo' rule	Text and graphics should be easy to read.	The text on your slides should be legible from a distance: don't strain the eyesight of your audience, unlike the short-sighted cartoon character Mr Magoo.
'Judging a book by its cover' rule	The form of your message should reflect its meaning.	Make sure that the background of your slides and any sounds are compatible with your text (hence, no loud noise effects for slides you will speak over).

Consider your conclusions

Plan a final slide that summarises your conclusions and any 'take home' message that you wish to convey to the audience. Express these conclusions in accordance with the 'rule of four' in Box 9.4.

Rehearse your talk
- Practise your talk to check that the number of slides you have prepared is appropriate for the length of time allocated to your talk.

- Visit the venue of your talk in advance.

- Find out if it's possible to test your slide presentation before the audience arrives.

Step 2: Giving your talk: Some 'dos and don'ts'

Do:
- Stand straight, act confidently and don't sway while speaking. State whether you'd prefer to have questions during your talk or after it.

- Dress comfortably and professionally based on your knowledge of the expectations of your audience and make an effort to look at the faces of your audience members – eye contact encourages a connection.

- Project your voice – speak loudly enough so that everyone in the room can hear what you're saying. Vary your tone of voice in a conversational way – don't speak in a monotonous drone.

- Speak slowly but steadily: racing though your slides is a sign of nervousness, so slow down. Adjust the pace of your delivery if your audience looks amused, puzzled or bored.

- Work on a strong ending – finish by summarising your key message.

Don't:
- Don't read your slides to the audience: listeners will 'tune out' because it's too difficult for them to read the slides while listening to your voice.

- Don't use jargon unless you're speaking to a specialist audience – and make sure that you can explain any technical terms in plain language.

- Don't apologise for your talk (e.g. 'Sorry, I hope this won't be too boring for you').

Managing your anxiety about giving a talk
If you need help to overcome anxiety before or during your presentation, here are some practical tips to consider.

Box 9.5 Practical tips for overcoming anxiety before or during your presentation

---

1 Prepare, prepare, prepare! The more organised you are, the more relaxed you will be when presenting.

2 Focus on what you can control – namely, your content and delivery. Don't engage in fortune-telling ('I wonder if they will like my talk?').

3 Remind yourself that the audience is interested and can learn from your talk.

4 Accept the fact that sometimes things can go wrong when you speak – but you can always do better the next time.

5 Use mental rehearsal to imagine yourself presenting your material successfully (see Box 6.4): see yourself standing tall in front of your audience, *hear* yourself speaking clearly and confidently, and *feel* yourself relaxing as you realise that your talk went well.

(See also Lightheart, 2016)

Step 3: Answering questions: Some 'dos and don'ts'

Do:

- Listen carefully to all parts of the question.

- If you're in a large or noisy room or if your questioner is in the front row, repeat the question aloud so that the entire audience can hear it.

- If you didn't hear or understand the question properly, politely ask the questioner to repeat it or to clarify what she or he meant.

- Pause before answering: it will give you time to think. If you don't know the answer, say so – don't bluff! If you think you will see the audience again (e.g. because you're giving a series of presentations), offer to look up the answer to tell them the next time, but make sure to keep your promise.

Don't:

- Don't be afraid to disagree politely with the questioner or to argue your point using appropriate supporting evidence.

- Don't be too defensive (e.g. 'My supervisor told me to do it that way'). This will make you seem immature.

- If you are asked a difficult question that you can't answer, thank the person who asked it. You can use this as a new research question: 'That's a very interesting angle that you've raised: I hadn't thought of it. Do you have any suggestions for us as to where it leads?'

- If you're using PowerPoint and are asked a question about a specific slide, just type the number of the slide in to your presentation when you're in slideshow mode and the programme will find that slide immediately.

PRACTICAL TIPS ON EFFECTIVE POSTER PRESENTATIONS

A poster presentation is a self-contained display that serves as an alternative to verbal presentations, especially at scientific conferences. It uses a mixture of text and graphics to describe a specific project from beginning to end. Normally, the author of the poster stands beside it during its scheduled display and answers questions about it from interested conference participants. Interestingly, poster presentations are increasingly being used in modules at undergraduate level.

The purpose of a poster presentation is to facilitate informal discussions of your work with other researchers. Therefore, the poster itself should be sufficiently eye-catching to attract the interest of people walking by. The main challenge of poster design, however, is the question of how to condense the story of your work into sections on a poster board that is about 1 metre high and about 1.5 metres wide (see also Northey & Timney, 2015).

- **Title**: Make it enticing, informative, short (fewer than ten words), clear, and accurate in portraying the content of the poster. A good tip here is to use a question that can attract the reader's attention. The title should be legible from a distance of up to two metres (font size 28–32).

- **Headings**: Typical headings for scientific posters include the introduction, which is usually the statement of the problem and hypotheses, the method, apparatus, results and conclusions.

- **Section headings**: Each section should include only essential information. Specific details and/or broader issues can be kept for informal discussion with the reader or observer.

- **Images**: Graphics should be relevant, simple and relate directly to your main message.

- **Text**: Use a *sans serif* font in mostly lower case. This font should be large enough (e.g. font size 28– 32) to read from a distance of one to two metres. Make sure that the text is larger than 24 point on an end product poster sheet (A0) and larger than 6 point on the A4 sheet summary of the poster. Include your name, affiliation, email address and the name of your supervisor on your poster.

- **Sequence**: Consider using numbers, letters, boxes or arrows to indicate the logical sequence in which the sections of the poster should be read.

- **Key message**: Include a final statement that succinctly summarises your most important findings. Use the one-minute rule: if a reader has only one minute to spare, will she or he understand your poster?

When you have finished your poster, ask yourself the following questions:

- Does the poster contain all essential information – and *only* such information?

- Is all of the information clear?

- Are all necessary sections included (e.g. a scientific poster should include the title, introduction, method, participants, procedure, results and conclusions)?

- Does each section provide a clear summary statement for that section that can be read at a glance?

- Is the sequence of information portrayed in an easy-to-follow and logical order?

- Have you prepared scaled-down versions to distribute to readers or observers if necessary (e.g. in A4)?

SUMMARY

In university, you will be expected to complete various academic assignments such as essays, papers, research projects and oral and poster presentations. These assignments are designed to develop your skills in marshalling evidence, drawing conclusions and in writing and presenting your ideas clearly and concisely to others, including classmates, conference participants and your professors. The purpose of this chapter was to provide some practical advice on planning, researching, writing and presenting your academic assignments.

In the first section, I presented some tips on planning your assignment such as how to specify your research question(s). Then, I gave you advice on how to gather and evaluate relevant research information for your assignment. The next section of the chapter contained tips on writing the first draft of your essay or paper, outlining why it's best to write your introduction last, not first. In the fourth section of the chapter, I provided rewriting and reviewing tips to help you to produce the final draft of your assignment. Finally, I presented key strategies to make effective oral presentations (talks) and poster presentations.

EXAMS TEST YOUR MEMORY, LIFE TESTS YOUR LEARNING; OTHERS WILL TEST YOUR PATIENCE.

Fennell Hudson (2017)

Chapter 10

Doing Your Best in Exams

Overcoming the Challenges of Assessment

INTRODUCTION

Since the early 1970s, research has shown that students' academic efforts are influenced greatly by their perception of the demands of the evaluation system being used (Snyder, 1971; Miller & Parlett, 1974). In short, *assessment* – not teaching – drives students' learning. Before you begin a course of study in university (I'll use the terms 'course' and 'module' interchangeably), you need to know exactly how and when you will be assessed, what marking criteria will be used, and when and in what format you will be required to submit your academic assignments (e.g. hardcopy or electronic). Although you may have done well academically in school, what do you really know about the challenges posed by the assessment system in university? For example, how should you revise for exams? What do examiners mean when they use certain words and phrases in exam questions? Are there any practical tips for doing well in multiple-choice question (MCQ) exams? What should you do on exam day, especially if you're nervous? The purpose of this chapter is to answer these and other relevant questions about doing your best when you're being assessed.

This chapter is organised as follows:

••

➤ I'll give you a brief overview of the types and functions of common assessment methods used in university.

➤ I'll explain how to prepare for, and do your best in, the assessment method of the exam including the unseen essay style and multiple-choice formats.

➤ I'll give you some practical tips on what to do and who to approach if you didn't do as well as you had expected in your exams.

••

ASSESSMENT METHODS IN UNIVERSITY: TYPES AND FUNCTIONS

'**Assessment**' is a systematic, evidence-based process in which your academic performance is evaluated in order to determine what knowledge and skills you have gained after a particular course of study. Ideally, this process involves four cyclical steps (Richmond, Boysen, & Gurung, 2016).

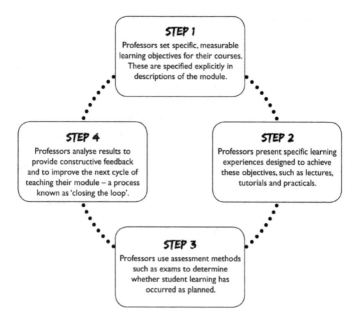

Figure 10.1: The four cyclical steps of university assessment

Assessment serves multiple functions in university. Firstly, it can help you to improve your knowledge and skills. In this regard, we need to distinguish between two kinds of assessment – *formative* and *summative*. The purpose of *formative* assessment, which usually takes place during a module, is to give you specific and constructive feedback designed to help you to improve your learning and understanding. You might be asked to submit a short plan for an essay, paper or research proposal that will be evaluated and commented on by your professor, who will then provide suggestions on how to improve it. By contrast, the purpose of *summative* assessment (e.g. a mid-term MCQ exam) is to determine how well you have actually learned what you were supposed to learn. Formative assessments don't normally contribute to your end-of-module grade but summative assessments always do.

A second function of assessment, especially summative, is to give you quantitative feedback such as a percentile rank on how your performance compares to that of your classmates at a particular point in time.

Finally, assessment is part of a wider process of 'quality assurance' in university education. This term refers to a commitment by university authorities to ensure that its academic standards are benchmarked and maintained according to specific international criteria. Put simply, assessment is a valuable tool for finding out if students have learned whatever they're required to know as part of their degree programmes.

Many different assessment methods are used in university. Box 10.1 presents a sample of these methods used in undergraduate studies.

Box 10.1 Common assessment methods in university

---

1 Traditional written exams (timed, unseen and often essay-style format)

2 Open book and open notes exams

3 MCQ exams

4 Essay or paper assignments

5 Independent research projects or theses or dissertations

6   Practical work (e.g. lab reports)

7   Portfolios

8   Presentations

9   Posters.

(Adapted from Race, Brown & Smith, 2005)

DOING YOUR BEST IN EXAMS

Assuming that you have attended class assiduously and studied effectively, how should you prepare for assessment? To do your best in exams, you need four key ingredients:

1   The right attitude

2   An effective revision plan

3   Good exam strategy

4   Knowledge of how to use your skills during the exam.

The right attitude: Exams as opportunities, not threats

The best way to look at exams is to regard them as opportunities *to show what you know* rather than as tests designed to find out what you *don't* know. This attitude has two major benefits. Firstly, it gives you something constructive to do before the exam – that is, to check that you *understand* and can *remember* what you have learned (see step 4 in the following revision tips). Secondly, it gives you confidence *during* the exam because it's comforting to know that you'll get credit from the examiners for every relevant piece of information that you write.

Unfortunately, many students fail to grasp this point, which is shown when they ask, 'Will I lose marks in an exam if I make a mistake?' This question incorrectly implies that you start with full marks in an exam but are penalised cumulatively for errors! In fact, the opposite is true. You start with zero marks in an exam but receive credit for all relevant and valid information that you provide subsequently. Put simply, examiners want to *give* you marks – not to take them away.

An effective revision plan

In Chapter 5, I explained the PQRR approach to reading. This technique emphasises the importance of reviewing or revising what you have learned in relation to your study questions. Accordingly, revision is not something you only do before important exams – it is an extension of the art of reading. The term 'revision' refers to a form of checking. More precisely, it involves reviewing your understanding of what you have learned. It does not mean either learning the material for the very first time or else trying to drum it into your mind by passive repetition.

Effective revision involves a sequence of four steps: reviewing the course; checking that you understand relevant course material (e.g. notes from lectures and books); summarising key points in the form of possible exam answers; and testing your ability to reproduce these outline answers under exam-like conditions.

Step 1: Review the scope of the course

In the first stage of your revision, the main objective is to obtain a quick overview of the course so that you can break it into sections or themes. This reorganisation of your course should be guided by the following questions.

What is the scope of the syllabus?

What topics on the course or module are examinable? Read all descriptions of the course outline and summary of the course online as well as any handouts that you received on the first day of class. If you have any doubts, ask your professors during office hours whether or not all the topics on the course are examinable.

What topics and questions have been examined in recent years?

A good way of understanding module requirements is to skim through typical questions that have been asked on it in recent years. Has the **exam rubric** changed from year to year? The exam rubric is the arrangement of the questions and any stipulations about the choices to be made. Is there any pattern evident in the type of questions that are asked regularly?

What is the best way to organise notes for each topic?

Classifying information is a useful way of preparing your mind to learn. Try to classify your notes by theme, using separate folders for all relevant lecture notes, module handouts, articles and other material such as textbook chapters for each section of the course.

Step 2: Check your understanding of course content

The next stage of revision involves checking your understanding of module content. Look for common themes in your notes. This strategy is helpful for two reasons. It reduces the amount of detail that you will have to remember and it makes you think about the academic material at a deeper, more abstract level. Both of these advantages will serve you well in exams. Having organised your notes, check your understanding of the material by approaching your professors during their office hours with specific questions about anything that's unclear to you. Don't wait until you're doing an exam to find out that you don't really understand the material as well as you thought.

Interestingly, people's revision attempts are often hampered by 'foresight bias' (Bjork et al., 2013) whereby students are over-confident that they will know something in a future exam because the information is in front of them while they're revising. This bias comes from a key difference between study and exam situations – that the answer is present during study but will be absent during the exam. Another useful revision strategy is to form a study group of classmates who will meet regularly to work on different topics. However, in order to achieve your learning goals (see Chapter 2), you must continue to study privately as well as work in groups.

Step 3: Make summary sheets to form answers to exam questions

When revising, create one-page summary sheets for each topic on the course (see also Chapter 5). These summaries provide skeletal answers to exam questions. For example, consider a past exam question in marine ecology such as 'Why should we conserve the marine environment and how would you evaluate the success of a marine conservation policy?'

Ideally, your summary notes should contain:

- A concise statement of the question underlying this topic, issue or theory (note that two questions are asked in the preceding example).

- Definitions of the key terms: 'conservation', 'marine environment' and 'conservation policy'.

- A list of important features or relevant research findings on the success or otherwise of marine conservation policies internationally.

- A list of strengths of relevant theories including points from other researchers including theories that inform typical marine conservation policies.

- A list of weaknesses of relevant theories including points from other researchers.

- Conclusions about what you have learned from research findings on marine conservation policy.

The questions that guide such summary sheets could come from key phrases from previous years' exam questions or else by inserting question marks after the titles of topics on the module syllabus. In the preceding example, the guiding question came from the key phrases 'conservation', 'marine environment' and 'conservation policy'.

Step 4: Test yourself under exam-like conditions (retrieval practice)
Test your ability to recall your summary sheets without your books or notes in front of you in simulated exam conditions. Research shows that frequent self-testing, or retrieval practice, strengthens memory for academic material (Putnam et al., 2016). Make sure to include an attempt to recall the main ideas from your summary sheet on a specific topic in every revision session. This can also be done quite easily while travelling on a bus or train or while waiting for a friend in a coffee shop. The more regularly you review your summary notes, the better your memory for them will be in an exam (see the principle of spaced or 'distributed practice' in Chapter 3).

Testing your skill in recalling summary sheets is beneficial for two reasons. It allows you to find out what you really know or can produce when you are forced to rely on your memory rather than on the notes that lie open in front of you. One of the biggest shocks that students can experience in an exam is the sudden discovery that they didn't know the material as well as they thought. Additionally, one of the best ways to counteract pressurised situations such as exams is to practise under conditions that simulate them. Some practical suggestions for testing yourself when revising are contained in Box 10.2.

Box 10.2 How to test yourself during revision

---

1 Using a blank sheet of paper, find out how much of your summary sheet you can recall. Note any discrepancies or inaccuracies carefully as these may be the points that you would omit in an exam.

2 Try solving a problem or exercise from your textbook and then compare your answer to that in the book.

3 Check your ability to define a technical concept without the aid of your notes. Then, compare your version with the definition in the textbook.

4 Cover up an important diagram in your textbook and see if you can reproduce it from memory alone.

Good exam strategy
The key to preparation is to have a good strategy for the periods before, during and after your exam.

The night before the exam
What should you do the night before an exam? Here are some practical tips.

Personal preparation

- Check the date, time and location of the exam. Make sure that you know what subject or which part of the course or module will be examined.

- Pack all your essential equipment for the exam into your bag (pens, pencils, ruler, calculator, and dictionary) and make sure to include some form of identification such as a student card and exam number. This identification may be required before you enter the exam hall.

- Decide what clothes to wear to the exam the following day. If possible, pick comfortable clothes that are light and layered.

Revision

- Glance over previous years' exam papers in this subject in order to get a flavour of the structure of the paper and the types of questions asked.

- Work out how many questions you will have to answer and how much time to allocate to each of them.

- Read over your summary sheets for each major topic or theme and test your ability to recall the material in them. Check that you can expand the abbreviations and acronyms that you use. For example, can you remember what the acronym PQRR stands for? (See Chapter 5).

- For each topic, make sure that you know what key points you wish to make about the topic and what evidence you can cite in support of them.

Rest

- Resist the temptation to study late into the night the evening before an exam. Last-minute cramming is not only exhausting, it can also lead to confusion and possible exam blanks the following day. Going for a relaxing walk is a useful thing to do the night before an exam.

- Set your alarm for the early morning so that you will have plenty of time to get ready for the exam. If you cannot fall asleep, or are tossing and turning all night, don't worry unduly. This restlessness simply means that you're concerned about your performance – which is a lot better than not caring at all! Your body is a self-correcting system that will restore your sleep balance over the next few nights.

- Never take sleeping pills or unprescribed medication the night before an exam. These drugs tend to make people feel groggy and lethargic the following day – hardly the ideal state of mind in which to sit an exam.

On the day of the exam

On the day of the exam, it's helpful to follow a definite routine that might include the following steps.

- Wake up early, freshen up with a shower and have a light but nourishing breakfast.

- Choose the clothes that you had planned to wear. Dress in layers of clothes that can be added to or removed conveniently depending on the temperature of the exam hall.

- Skim swiftly through your condensed notes or summary sheets: there's no need to read new material.

- Check that you've packed all your exam materials into your bag.

- Make your way to the exam hall so that you will arrive about 20–30 minutes before the exam starts. This period of time is long enough to enable you to become accustomed to the exam atmosphere but short enough to prevent you from becoming overwhelmed by the anxiety of anticipating the exam.

- If it makes you relax, you may wish to have a chat with some of your classmates or else review your summary sheets again. Normally, it's not a good idea to review textbooks at this stage because they are too detailed.

Managing anxiety before your exams

It's natural to feel some anxiety or apprehension about the future before an exam. Feeling tense, having a racing heartbeat and feeling butterflies in your stomach are just bodily signs that you *care* about what you're about to do. In such situations, your brain primes your body for action by releasing hormones such as adrenaline into your bloodstream (the 'fight or flight' response). This surge of energy increases your readiness to face what you fear.

How can you make your nervous energy work *for* you rather than *against* you? Well, as most anxiety arises from a fear of the unknown, it's vital to take as much control as possible over your exam situation. This can be done in two ways.

- Familiarise yourself with the nature and location of the exam. Check out the exam hall in advance so that you're familiar with its layout and atmosphere.

- Learn to control *your own* behaviour and to ignore what other people do during the exam. Remember the advice of Usain Bolt in Chapter 6: *run your own race*. Don't look around you in the exam hall when the papers are handed out and don't pay any attention to students who request extra paper from the invigilators.

If your anxiety persists beyond the exam period, then it may be helpful to discuss your problems with an approachable professor or a study skills adviser in your university. Asking for professional help is an important step in solving any problem.

How to use your skills during the exam

Under the stress of exams, people often forget to perform intended actions. The best antidote to this problem is to follow a consistent routine as much as possible in the exam hall. Adhering to a routine is beneficial because it will focus your mind on the task to be done – not on any doubts or worries that may be at the back of your mind. The key words in this routine are: reading, planning, writing and checking.

Before walking into the exam hall, make sure that you are not carrying any exam notes with you. Leave them outside the hall – otherwise you may be accused of cheating. Also, it is a good idea to visit the toilet – three hours is a long time! Next, find your exam desk, sit down and lay out your pens, pencils and identification card in front of you. Look for the clock. If you cannot see it, you should leave your watch down on the desk in a visible location so that you can consult it easily during the exam. Then, take a few deep breaths and say to yourself, 'This is an opportunity to show what I've learned. I've prepared well for this moment and I'm going to keep writing until the exam is over.' Wait for any announcements to be made and for the exam papers to be distributed to you. Most essay-type exams have a three-hour time limit and 3–4 questions to be answered. In order to do your best in this situation, you must have a plan for using your time efficiently. Here are some suggestions for what to do after you have received your paper.

The first 5 minutes

- Be glad that you are feeling slightly anxious. Remember that nervous excitement is a sign that your body is 'revved up' and ready to perform.

- Check that you have received the correct exam paper. Sometimes mistakes can occur at this stage, so be attentive.

- Keep your head down and focus only on your own behaviour. Don't allow yourself to be distracted by the sights and sounds around you: run your own race.

- Write your name or student number and details on your script.

- Pay special attention to the rubric (instructions at the top of the paper) specifying the number of questions that you are obliged to answer. Are there are any questions on the reverse side of the paper? Sometimes, in the heat of the moment, anxious students may forget to turn over the paper. Establish which of the questions are optional and which ones are compulsory.

- Spend 3–5 minutes reading the entire paper from beginning to end. You'll probably experience a mixture of surprise and relief when you see the paper. The surprise may come from the absence of certain topics that you had prepared for and had expected to appear on the paper. Hopefully, you'll be relieved to find out that certain familiar topics have been included in the questions. Be careful to read the precise question being asked about these topics. If you are anxious and 'primed' to see a topic that you had prepared, there is a danger that you will rush headlong into it without taking into account the examiners' angle on the question. To overcome this problem, *underline each key word* in the questions that you select.

- Decide which questions to tackle first. Normally, it's better to start with the question that you know most about and to leave the most difficult one until last.

- Underline key words in each of your selected questions to make sure that you fully understand what's expected of you and to ensure that what you write is consistently relevant to your answer. If possible, try to allocate a different paragraph to each of the key words in your answer.

- Put a finishing time beside each question to prevent you from spending too long on it.

- Write the number of the question you are answering clearly at the top of the page. Don't waste any time in copying out the text of question at the top of your answer.

Main exam time

- Answer the question that you were *actually* asked – not the one that you would *like* to have been asked! Some students fall into the trap of saying to themselves, 'I've spent a long time preparing this topic so the examiner is going to get all of my prepared answer to it – no matter what the question is!'

- Your task in an exam is not to summarise the notes that you have lying outside the exam hall but, instead, to use your notes as the scaffolding on which to build your answer. Therefore, you must respond to the wording of the question. The trick here is to weave your prepared answer into the questions asked. In other words, most good answers in an exam are a blend of prepared material (specifically, the skeleton summary sheets that you have used in your revision) and thinking on the spot. The trap to avoid in this regard is neglecting key words in the questions and presenting a pre-packaged but largely irrelevant answer.

- If a question has several different parts, make sure that you cover each one as well as possible.

- To ensure that you stick to the point, jot down any relevant ideas you can think of and make a brief plan at the beginning of your answer. Although it's tempting to write a hasty answer to any question that seems vaguely familiar (especially since other students always seem to be able to write faster than you do!), it pays to spend a little time in planning your answer. Plans remind you of key points to include in your answer. In addition, they'll reduce your likelihood of wandering off the point.

- Try to answer the question from different perspectives, allocating a separate paragraph for each point. This format allows the marker(s) to see each point clearly and facilitates marking.

- Check your progress regularly by making sure that you are sticking to your 'answer plan'.

- If possible, use short sentences when writing. This habit reduces the likelihood of making mistakes that confuse both you and the examiners.

- To write coherent paragraphs, you need to link your ideas together. For this purpose, use transition (signpost) words that bridge the gaps between one sentence and another. Useful transition words are 'similarly', 'to illustrate', 'for example', 'to explain' and 'in summary'.

- Include a critical evaluation of the material as often as possible, supported by appropriate evidence or arguments. This evaluation may take the form of questioning assumptions or methods or comparing and contrasting rival theories.

- If you include any diagrams or graphs, make sure that they are labelled clearly. Failure to indicate what the diagram means suggests a lack of understanding of the material.

- Keep checking that you have not exceeded your proposed finishing time for your answer. If you go beyond the budgeted time, leave a reasonable space and begin the next question. You can always come back to the unfinished one later.

- Try to keep your writing clear and legible.

- If you need more paper, raise your non-writing hand and wait for the invigilator to come down to your desk.

The final 5 minutes

- Keep writing and stay in the exam hall until you are asked to stop. Sit at your desk until the invigilator collects your paper. Check that your name and exam number are clearly indicated on the answer script.

- If you finish before the exam is over, then review your work to see if there is anything else you can add to your answers.

- Always hand up your 'rough work' in an exam. The notes that it contains may gain additional marks for you.

A list of typical words and phrases used in exams together with their meaning is provided in Box 10.3.

Box 10.3 What do the examiners want? Decoding the meaning of exam questions

In order to perform well in examinations, you must answer the question that you have been asked. What exactly do examiners want you to do when they use certain words and phrases? Here is a glossary of 'exam language' (based on Cottrell, 2017; Dembo & Selli, 2016; Hayes & Stratton, 2017).

Phrasing	What you are being asked to do
Compare and contrast	Write about both the similarities ('compare') and the differences ('contrast') between two or more things.
Critically evaluate	Write about the strengths and weaknesses of the theory or topic in question. Refer to criticisms by other researchers (cite authors or year). If possible, give your own view but make sure it's supported by relevant evidence.
Define	Explain the precise meaning of a given term or phrase.
Describe	Give a detailed account of the topic in simple language. Leave your own ideas to the last paragraph – but always provide evidence to support them.
Discuss	Write about the details of your topic from all sides of the issue and/or using different points of view. Provide positive and negative points as advantages or disadvantages.
Evaluate or review	Assess the worth of something. Examine both sides of the issue or argument. Assess the strengths and weaknesses of the topic. Include your own views substantiated with evidence.
Examine	Analyse the topic or question as if you were putting it under a microscope. Also, critically evaluate it.
Explain	Give reasons and/or evidence to support your account of the topic.
Give an account of	Describe the topic in detail (see 'describe').
Illustrate	Make something clear and explicit by giving specific examples or evidence.
Interpret	Clarify the meaning of something by giving its meaning as you see it.
List	Present relevant information in a numbered sequence.
Outline	Describe the main facts (e.g. definitions, characteristics) to make the topic easy to understand.
State	Present the main features of something.
Summarise	Provide a concise account of the main points.
Support	Back up what you write by providing relevant evidence (e.g. research findings).
Trace	Begin with a definition of the topic or issue and describe key events on its history.

What if you run out of time?

As time is a precious commodity in an exam, it must be budgeted carefully. What should you do if you spend too long on one question and are now running out of time? The only solution here is to write brief notes that provide an elaboration of your answer plan. If necessary, you could also direct the attention of the examiner to any notes you may have included in any rough work sheets that you worked on during the exam. Make sure to hand up these sheets as well as any other official exam material. If you write notes for an answer, try to explain key points as concisely as possible. Under no circumstances should you waste time in writing such phrases as 'I have no time left'! These phrases are not only a waste of valuable time (as they're not relevant to the content of your answer) but may also irritate your examiners.

Before I conclude this section, it's important to explore the main reasons why students fail exams. If you know these pitfalls in advance, you can learn to avoid them.

WHY DO STUDENTS FAIL EXAMS?

Some of the most common reasons for failure are listed in Box 10.4.

Box 10.4 Exams: Common pitfalls to avoid

Students fail exams for many reasons. The most common of these difficulties are listed below. Make sure that you don't fall into any of these exam traps.

1 Inadequate preparation – not having enough knowledge to answer the questions asked.

2 Not reading the exam question(s) correctly (e.g. rushing into a question without considering its wording or context).

3 Failing to answer the required number of questions (e.g. leaving a 'blank' on an exam script or providing an answer that is too short and superficial).

4 Irrelevance or failing to answer the question asked (e.g. ignoring certain key words in the exam question, including quotations that are not relevant to the question under discussion, failing to provide sufficient evidence to support arguments).

5 Inability to apply what one has learned in the course, that is, showing no evidence of understanding basic principles explained in lectures or reading.

6 Excessive repetition: making the same point again and again does not merit extra marks.

7 Inefficient use of exam time by spending too long on one question.

8 Poor presentation of work with a sloppy and disorganised appearance of text, no paragraphs, rambling sentences, presenting abbreviated notes only.

9 Not finishing the paper or leaving before the exam is over. Remember – you can only get marks for what you write down!

In summary, this section has provided some practical advice on what to do and what not to do when sitting exams. Let's now consider how to manage MCQ exams.

MANAGING MCQ EXAMS

Multiple choice exams typically present a stem statement containing an incomplete sentence or question below which is a choice of four alternative answers. Only one of these choices or options is correct. Because of their format, MCQ exams test your *recognition* rather than your recall skills.

Here are some practical tips on answering MCQs (based on Dembo & Seli, 2016; Northey & Timney, 2015).

The first 5 minutes
- Read the instructions carefully. How many choices can you make – just one or more than one? Are there penalties for guessing?

- How many questions do you have to answer? You usually have to answer all of them.

- Budget for time: if there are 30 questions and you have 50 minutes, then you have approximately 90 seconds per item, so don't dwell too long on any one item.

Main exam time

- Read the question carefully, paying special attention to words or phrases like 'not' (e.g. 'Which of the following is *not* a . . .').

- If you see a 'no' in the stem, circle it and read the stem again to make sure that you understand it correctly.

- Attempt the easy questions first and come back to the difficult ones later.

- Don't read too much into the questions – MCQ test makers usually don't try to be deceptive.

- If possible, try to determine the correct answer *before* looking at the options available: if you can't do so, read the stem of each question along with each possible option to see if any of them jog your memory.

- Eliminate any unlikely answers from the options available to you.

- Identify what you think is the correct answer.

- Re-read the question and apply the stem to your preferred option to make sure that the sentence or answer seems correct: sometimes this strategy validly allows you to eliminate ungrammatical sentences.

- If there are no penalties for guessing, then guess rather than leaving a blank answer.

- Ignore superstitions. Don't waste any time in looking for patterns in the options. For example, it's just as possible for four 'd' options in a row to be correct as it is for the options to be otherwise distributed.

The final 5 minutes

- If you have time, review your answers before you hand in your exam.

AFTER THE EXAM: POST-MORTEMS

Although it's very tempting at the time, there is little to be gained by doing post-mortems with your classmates on exams that have been completed. As you can't change the past, there is little point in torturing yourself by reminding yourself about what might have been or what you *should* have included in your answer. Also, you're probably not a good judge of the quality of what you wrote in the exam. Indeed, most students are inaccurate in their recall of what they *actually* wrote. Therefore, your worries about what you wrote in an exam are rarely justified by the facts. Nevertheless, it's natural for you to want to know what your classmates thought of the exam and how they performed in it. So, by all means, exchange a few words with them about the test, but avoid a detailed question-by-question analysis of the paper because it's only likely to cause you to regret possible mistakes or omissions.

Perhaps the best thing to do after an exam is to take some gentle physical exercise which will help you to 'warm down' after the intense experience of answering questions under time pressure. Later, you may wish to focus on the next paper to be tackled in your exams. Remember – concentrate on one exam at a time. Don't look too far ahead or you may become downhearted.

Learning from results: 'I did worse than I had expected'

One of the paradoxes of university life is that students often exper-ience a sense of anti-climax rather than relief when they finish their exams. Usually, this feeling stems from a combination of cumulative fatigue and a failure to plan routine activities beyond the exam period. Sooner or later, you'll get your exam results. What should you do if the results are disappointing?

The most important point to understand is that exam results are a source of *feedback* on your performance on a particular occasion rather than an infallible diagnosis of your academic ability for the rest of your life. Therefore, you *can* improve your academic performance – if you're prepared to *seek advice* from your professors or faculty as soon as your results become available. Here are some suggestions for this task.

- Establish as much factual information as possible about your exam results including your marks on each section or paper and clarify the options that are open to you. Do you have to repeat the module concerned or is compensation possible?

- Find out how soon you can repeat any exam(s) that you have failed. Do you have to register officially for these repeat exams in the university?

- Ask your academic school or department if it's possible to look at your exam script. Many universities have formal periods after exams during which scripts may be viewed under staff supervision.

- Ask your professors for advice about how to improve your academic performance in the light of your exam results.

- Do your professors recommend that you should seek tutorial help from a postgraduate student in the department or school? If so, would they be able to recommend someone suitable to you?

- If you're not happy with the feedback that you received from your academic department or school, it may be helpful to contact the Education Officer of the Students' Union in your university.

Sometimes the disappointment of exam results comes not from being blocked temporarily from some career-relevant path or decision but from social comparison processes. In short, you may feel despondent simply because you did worse than your friends or classmates. Although this feeling is understandable, especially if they seem to have done less study for the exams than you did, it's not helpful because you should focus only on what you can control – not on what happens to someone else. In any case, you must be prepared to take responsibility for your failures as well as your successes. It is up to you whether you regard results as a temporary setback or as a final judgement on you as a person.

Extenuating circumstances

Sometimes students perform significantly below their ability in modules due to ill-health, bereavement, accidents or other such difficult circumstances. 'Extenuating circumstances' are any unforeseen factors beyond your control that may have prevented you from satisfying the requirements of your academic programme (e.g. during exams or in submission of prescribed assignment). These factors include:

- An acute illness or a serious ongoing medical condition

- Acute or ongoing serious personal or emotional circumstances

- Ongoing, life-threatening illness of a close family member or partner

- Bereavement of a close family member or partner

- Involvement in an accident

- Being the victim of a crime

- Domestic upheaval at the time of the assessment (e.g. fire, burglary, eviction).

If you believe that any of these circumstances may have affected your academic performance adversely during a module, then it's important to seek advice from office staff in your academic department or school, relevant professors, the Students' Union, student advisers, chaplains or your degree Programme Office before submitting a formal application to the university.

SUMMARY

It has long been known that *assessment* – not teaching – drives students' learning. Before you begin any module, you need to know exactly how and when you will be assessed, what marking criteria will be used, and when and in what format you will be required to submit your academic assignments. What do you really know about the challenges posed by the assessment system in university? The purpose of this chapter was to give you some practical tips on doing your best when you're being assessed.

I began with a brief overview of the types and functions of some common assessment methods used in university. Then, I explained how to prepare for and do your best in exams – perhaps the most popular of these methods. Exams can include the unseen essay style and multiple choice formats. More precisely, I suggested that exam success depends on four main factors.

1 Having the right attitude (i.e. seeing exams as opportunities to show what you know – not tests designed to find out what you *don't* know).

2 Having an effective revision plan.

3 Having a good exam strategy (what to do the night before the exam and how to deal with question choice and time management issues during it).

4 Using your skills in remembering, explaining and applying relevant knowledge during the exam.

I then went on to provide practical tips covering each of these factors. This section of the chapter also included practical advice on how to test yourself during revision – 'retrieval practice' – on understanding what exactly examiners want you to do when they use certain words or phrases in exam questions, and on handling MCQ exams. The chapter concluded with practical tips on what to do and who to approach if you didn't do as well as you had expected in your exams

A final word: A life of learning

Now that you have explored the challenge of managing your own learning in university, two new challenges arise. The first of these challenges is to continue to *think for yourself* (see Chapter 7) in every area of your life – from the classroom to the workplace. Remember, as Bloom et al. (2017) proposed, the main objective of a university education is to seek truth and to learn the skills and fortitude required to be a lifelong truth-seeker. Your second challenge concerns wholehearted engagement with university life. This involves making your time in university as memorable as possible so that you can look back on it in years to come and say 'I loved every minute of it because I gave it everything I had!'

Glossary

Chapter 1

cognition　　　　　　　Mental processes, like thinking, by which people acquire, store and use their knowledge

cognitive　　　　　　　Relating to 'cognition', i.e. relating to mental processes, like thinking, by which people acquire, store and use their knowledge

cognitive psychologist　　A person who undertakes the scientific study of mental processes such as thinking

comprehension monitoring　　Checking the degree and quality of your understanding as you read a passage of text

conceptual knowledge　　Knowledge about things: facts, rules, principles and relationships

deliberate learning　　Learning that is active, purposeful and effortful

incidental learning　　Learning that is unplanned or implicit

learning　　A relatively permanent change in knowledge, understanding or behaviour that results from experience

metacognition　　People's knowledge about, and control over, their own cognitive processes

metacognitive　　Relating to 'metacognition', i.e. relating to people's knowledge about, and control over, their own cognitive processes

procedural skills　　Knowing how to do things, such as the steps required to perform a task or achieve a goal

self-reference effect　　The discovery that the act of relating information to yourself increases the information's memorability

Chapter 2

deliberate practice   A purposeful, focused and systematic effort to improve the skills that one cannot perform well, or at all, at present

displacement activities   Delaying tactics and self-created distractions that hamper your attempts to start a task

generic practice   Mechanical practice characterised by the relatively mindless repetition of skills that you can already perform quite well

grit   A popular term for making a commitment to finish what you start, to bounce back from setbacks (resilience), and to exert a sustained effort in practising things that you are not good at in order to achieve success

law of effect   The discovery that any behaviour that leads to a satisfying state of affairs is likely to occur again, whereas any behaviour that leads to an annoying state of affairs is less likely to occur again

Chapter 3

cramming   Also known as 'massed practice': studying infrequently for long periods of time

hippocampus   A brain structure that plays a central role in learning and memory

monotasking   Doing just one thing for a given length of time

procrastination   The habit of voluntarily postponing an important task that you intend to do despite knowing that you'll suffer more and perform worse as a consequence

Chapter 4

augmented reality   A form of digital technology that provides layers of computer-generated enhancements on top of reality in order to facilitate interaction with it

distributed practice   Studying material regularly and briefly; also known as 'spaced practice'

memory	A brain process that enables us to store, organise and retrieve our knowledge, experiences and skills
phonological loop	'Inner voice' or the component of the working memory system that is responsible for maintaining speech sounds for a second or two
virtual learning environment	Online system(s) that facilitate(s) digital teaching and learning activities
virtual reality	An artificial, computer-generated simulation of a real-life environment or situation

Chapter 5
constructive activity	The act of understanding the meaning of a text as you read

Chapter 6
cognitive overload	The experience of being overwhelmed with information
means-end analysis	A strategy which involves breaking a problem into smaller tasks or sub-goals in order to solve it
pre-performance routines	Preferred sequences of preparatory thoughts and actions that performers use in an effort to concentrate effectively before the execution of key skills
working memory	A mental system that controls our ability to hold information in our minds for short periods of time while we work on it

Chapter 7
active reflection	Working things out for oneself
neuroscience	The study of how brain systems give rise to mental processes
primary sources	Immediate, first-hand accounts of a topic
secondary sources	Material, such as a textbook, that interprets a primary source

Chapter 8
meaningful learning   High-level thinking in which one tries to under-
                           stand concepts and to apply them to new situations

mnemonic   A practical memory aid

overlearning   A form of practice or learning characterised by
                           continuing beyond the point at which one already
                           knows the material well

retrieval practice effect   Testing yourself regularly to find out if you can
                                 retrieve what you have learned improves your
                                 long-term memory

storage   The representation and retention of information
                           in the memory system

Chapter 9
plagiarism   The inclusion of another person's writing or
                           ideas in any formally presented work that forms
                           part of the requirements of a module without
                           due acknowledgement or citation of the original
                           source of the material

primacy effect   The discovery that items presented first in a
                           sequence tend to be remembered better than
                           those presented in the middle

recency effect   The discovery that items presented last in a
                           sequence tend to be remembered better than
                           those presented in the middle

Chapter 10
exam rubric   The formal instruction from the examiners about
                           the arrangement of exam questions and any
                           stipulations about the choices/options on the
                           exam paper

References

Abbott, E. E. (1909). On the analysis of the factors of recall in the learning process. *Psychological Monographs*, 11. (pp. 159–177).

Adams Becker, S., et al. (2017). NMV Horizon Report: 2017 Higher Education Edition. 7 July 2018. <https://www.nmc.org/publication/nmc-horizon-report-2017-higher-education-edition/>.

Ahern, L., J. Feller, & T. Nagle. (2016). Social media as a support for learning in universities: An empirical study of Facebook Groups. *Journal of Decision Systems*, 25. (pp. 35–49).

Alter, A. (2017). *Irresistible: The Rise of Addictive Technology and the Business of Keeping Us Hooked*. New York: Penguin Press.

Annett, J. (1991). Skill acquisition. In J. E. Morrison (Ed.), *Training for Performance: Principles of Applied Human Learning* (pp. 13–51). Chichester: John Wiley.

Atkinson, R. C., & R. M. Shiffrin. (1968). Human memory: A proposed system and its control processes. In K. W. S. Spence & J. T. Spence (Eds.). *The Psychology of Learning and Motivation* (pp. 89–105). New York: Academic Press.

Bartlett, F. (1958). *Thinking: An Experimental and Social Study*. London: Allen and Unwin.

Beyerstein, B. L. (1999). Whence cometh the myth that we only use 10% of our brains? In S. D. Sala (Ed.), *Mind Myths: Exploring Popular Assumptions About the Mind and Brain* (pp. 3–24). Chichester: John Wiley.

Bhalia, J. (8 May 2013). It is in our nature to need stories. *Scientific American*. 9 June 2018. <https://blogs.scientificamerican.com/guest-blog/it-is-in-our-nature-to-need-stories/>.

Bjork, E. L., & R. A. Bjork. (2011). Making things hard on yourself, but in a good way: Creating desirable difficulties to enhance learning. In M. A. Gernsbacher, et al. (Eds.). *Psychology and the Real World: Essays Illustrating Fundamental Contributions to Society* (pp. 56–64). New York: Worth Publishers.

Bjork, R. A. et al. (2013). Self-regulated learning: Beliefs, techniques, and illusions. *Annual Review of Psychology*, 74. (pp. 417–444).

Bloom, P. et al. (29 Aug. 2017). Some thoughts and advice for our students and all students. 28 May 2018. <https://jmp.princeton.edu/announcements/some-thoughts-and-advice-our-students-and-all-students>.

Bransford, J. D., & M. K. Johnson. (1972). Contextual prerequisites for understanding: Some investigations of comprehension and recall. *Journal of Verbal Learning and Verbal Behaviour*, 11. (pp. 717–26).

Bradbury, N. A. (2016). Attention span during lectures: 8 seconds, 10 minutes, or more? *Advances in Physiology Education*, 40. (pp. 509–513).

Brolin, C. (2017). *In the Zone: How Champions Think and Win Big*. London: Blink Publishing.

Brockwell, P. (12 July 2016). Being a mother is irrelevant to a woman's ability to do the (top) job. *The Guardian*. 30 May 2018. <https://www.theguardian.com/commentisfree/2016/jul/12/mother-top-job-andrea-leadsom-theresa-may>.

Browne, M. N., & S. M. Keeley. (2014). *Asking the Right Questions: A Guide to Critical Thinking* (11th ed.). Boston: Pearson.

Burgess, A. (1966). *New York Times Book Review*, 4 December.

Burnett, D. (2017). *The Idiot Brain: A Neuroscientist Explains What Your Head is Really Up To*. London: Guardian Faber.

Butler, G., N. Grey & T. Hope. (2018). *Manage Your Mind* (3rd ed.). Oxford: Oxford University Press.

Butler, H. A., C. Pentoney, & M. Bong. (2017). Predicting real-world outcomes: Critical thinking is a better predictor of life decisions than intelligence. *Thinking Skills and Creativity*, 25. (pp. 38–46).

Carter, S. B. (4 Jan. 2012). The power of the mind: Quotes to get you thinking. *Psychology Today*. 28 July 2018. <https://www.psychologytoday.com/gb/blog/high-octane-women/201201/the-power-the-mind-quotes-get-you-thinking>.

Chen, Y. (2016). The effects of virtual reality learning environment on student cognitive and linguistic development. *The Asia-Pacific Education Researcher*, 25. (pp. 637–646).

Collins. (1996). *Collins Concise Dictionary of Quotations*. Glasgow: Harper Collins.

Cottrell, S. (2017). Critical Thinking Skills (3rd ed.). London: Palgrave Macmillan.

Cottrell, S., & N. Morris. (2012). *Study Skills Connected: Using Technology to Support Your Studies*. London: Palgrave Macmillan.

Craik, F. I. M., & R. S. Lockhart. (1972). Levels of processing: A framework for memory research. *Journal of Verbal Learning and Verbal Behaviour*, 11. (pp. 671–684).

Crawley, P. (21 May 2015). Opening the Gate: Is Irish theatre still talking to itself? *The Irish Times*. (p. 13).

Creswell, J. D. (2017). Mindfulness interventions. *Annual Review of Psychology*, 68. (pp. 491–516).

Davis, B. G. (2009). *Tools for Teaching*. San Francisco, CA: Jossey–Bass.

D'Esposito, M., & B. R. Postle. (2015) The cognitive neuroscience of working memory. *Annual Review of Psychology*, 66. (pp. 115–142).

de Sousa, A. F., et al. (2018). The influence of exercise and physical fitness status on attention: A systematic review. *International Review of Sport & Exercise Psychology*. In press.

Deem, J. (1993). *Study Skills in Practice*. Boston: Houghton Mifflin.

Dekker, S., et al. (2012). Neuromyths in education: Prevalence and predictors of misconceptions among teachers. *Frontiers in Psychology*, 3 : 429.

Dembo, M. H., & H. Seli. (2016). *Motivation and Learning Strategies for College Success: A Focus on Self–Regulated Learning*. London: Routledge.

Dewey, J. (1933). *How We Think: A Restatement of the Relation of Reflective Thinking to the Education Process*. Boston: Heath.

Dewey, J. (1944). *Democracy and Education*. New York: Macmillan.

Di Domenico, S. I., & R. M. Ryan. (2017). The emerging neuroscience of intrinsic motivation: A new frontier in self-determination research. *Frontiers in Human Neuroscience*, 11 : 145.

Doebel, S., & Y. Munakata. (2018). Group influences on engaging self-control: Children delay gratification and value it more when their in-group delays and their out-group doesn't. *Psychological Science*, in press.

Dolan, R. (2017). Effective presentation skills. *FEMS Microbiology Letters*, *364*. (pp. 1–3).

Dooling, D. J., & R. Lachman. (1971). Effects of comprehension on retention of prose. *Journal of Experimental Psychology*, 88. (pp. 216–22).

Dunlosky, J., et al. (2013). Improving students' learning with effective learning techniques: Promising directions from cognitive and educational psychology. *Psychological Science in the Public Interest*, 14. (pp. 4–58).

Duckworth, A. (2017). *Grit: Why Passion and Resilience are the Secrets to Success*. London: Vermilion.

Ebbinghaus, H. (1885/1964). *Memory: A Contribution to Experimental Psychology*. New York: Dover.

Erickson, K. I., et al. (2011). Exercise training increases size of hippocampus and improves memory. *Proceedings of the National Academy of Sciences*, 108. (pp. 3017–3022).

Ericsson, A., & R. Pool. (2017). *Peak: How All of Us Can Achieve Extraordinary Things*. London: Vintage.

Ericsson, K. A., R. T. Krampe, & C. Tesch-Romer. (1993). The role of deliberate practice in the acquisition of expert performance. *Psychological Review*, 100. (pp. 363–406).

Eysenck, M. W., & M. T. Keane. (2015). *Cognitive Psychology: A Student's Handbook* (7th ed.). London: Psychology Press.

Fabritius, F., & H. W. Hagemann. (2017). *The Leading Brain*. New York: Tarcher/Perigee.

Farrelly, T., Raftery, D., & Harding, N. (2018). Exploring lecturer engagement with the VLE: Findings from a multi-college staff survey. *Irish Journal of Technology Enhanced Learning*, 3. (pp. 11-23).

Foer, J. (2011). *Moonwalking with Einstein: The Art and Science of Remembering Everything*. New York: Penguin.

Forshaw, M. (2012). *Critical Thinking for Psychology: A Student Guide*. Chichester, West Sussex: BPS Blackwell.

Forster, E.M. (1956). *Aspects of the Novel*. Mariner Books.

Freeman, S., et al. (2014). Active learning increases student performance in science, engineering, and mathematics. *Proceedings of the National Academy of Sciences (USA)*, 111. (pp. 8410–8415).

Gallo, C. (2014). The science behind TED's 18-minute rule. 12 May 2018. <https://www.linkedin.com/pulse/20140313205730-5711504-the-science-behind-ted-s-18-minute-rule>.

Gazzaniga, M. (2018). *Psychological Science* (6th ed.). New York: W. W. Norton.

Gilovich, T. (1991). *How We Know What Isn't So: The Fallibility of Human Reason in Everyday Life*. New York: The Free Press.

Gladwell, M. (2009). *Outliers: The Story of Success*. London: Penguin.

Godden, D. R., & A. D. Baddeley. (1975). Context-dependent memory in two natural environments: on land and underwater. *British Journal of Psychology*, 66. (pp. 325–332).

Goodwin, D. W., et al. (1969). Alcohol and recall: state-dependent effects in man. *Science*, 163. (pp. 1358–1360).

Goldstein, E. (2011). *Cognitive Psychology* (3rd ed.). Belmont, CA: Wadsworth/ Cengage.

Gruber, M. J., at al. (2014). States of curiosity modulate hippocampus-dependent learning via the dopaminergic circuit. *Neuron*, 84. (pp. 486–496).

Gruneberg, M. (1987). *Linkword French, German, Spanish, Italian, Greek, Portuguese*. London: Corgi.

Gruneberg, M. M., & G. D. Jacobs. (1991). In defence of linkwords. *The Language Learning Journal*, 3. (pp. 25–29).

Hamblin, T. J. (1981). Fake. *British Medical Journal*, 283. (pp. 1671–1675).

Harley, J. M., et al. (2016). Comparing virtual and location-based augmented reality mobile learning: Emotions and learning outcomes. *Educational Technology, Research and Development*, 64. (pp. 359–388).

Hayes, N., & P. Stratton. (2017). *A Student's Dictionary of Psychology and Neuroscience* (6th ed.). London: Routledge.

Heisz, J. J., et al. (2017). The effects of physical exercise and cognitive training on memory and neurotrophic factors. *Journal of Cognitive Neuroscience*, 29. (pp. 1895–1907).

Henderson, M., et al. (2015). Students' everyday engagement with digital technology in university: Exploring patterns of use and 'usefulness'. *Journal of Higher Education Policy and Management*, 37(3). (pp. 308–319).

Herlevich, N. E. (1990). Reflecting on old Olympus' towering tops. Journal of Ophthalmic Nursing Technology, 9. (pp. 245-246).

Higher Education Authority. (2015). *National Employer Survey: Employers' Views on Irish Further and Higher Education and Training Outcomes.* Dublin: Higher Education Authority.

Hoffield, D. (2017). Want to know what your brain does when it hears a question? 19 May 2018. <https://www.fastcompany.com/3068341/want-to-know-what-your-brain-does-when-it-hears-a-question>.

Hoffman, R. J. (2014). The Wall by Jean-Paul Sartre. 29 July 2018. <https://romanjameshoffman.wordpress.com/2014/12/27/the-wall-by-jean-paul-sartre/>.

Hudson, Fennel. (2017). *A Writer's Year: Fennel's Journal No. 3.* Clwyd: Fennel's Priory Limited.

Husmann, P. R., & V. D. O'Loughlin. (2018). Another nail in the coffin for learning styles? Disparities among undergraduate anatomy students' study strategies, class performance, and reported VARK learning styles. *Anatomical Sciences Education,* in press.

James, W. (1890). The Principles of Psychology (Vol 1). Cambridge, Mass: Harvard University Press.

James, W. (1890). *Talks to Teachers on Psychology: And to Students on Some of Life's Ideas.* New York: Henry Holt and Company. <http://ebooks.adelaide.edu.au/j/james/williams/talks/>.

Kahneman, D. (2011). *Thinking, Fast and Slow.* London: Allen Lane.

Kosslyn, S. M. (2011). *Better PowerPoint: Quick Fixes Based on How Your Audience Thinks.* Oxford: Oxford University Press.

Lannin, D. G., & N. A. Scott. (2014). Best practices for an online world. *American Psychological Association.* 26 July 2018. <http://www.apa.org/monitor/2014/02/ce-corner.aspx>.

Lennox, G. (17 June 2018). Shakes on a plane (InGear). *The Sunday Times.* (pp. 27–28).

Leslie, I. (2014). *Curious: The Desire to Know and Why Your Future Depends on It.* New York: Basic Books.

Lightheart, A. (2016). *Presentation Now: Prepare a Perfect Presentation in Less Than 3 Hours.* Harlow: Pearson.

Lilienfeld, S. O., et al. (2009). *50 Great Myths of Popular Psychology: Shattering Widespread Misconceptions About Human Behaviour.* New York: Wiley-Blackwell.

Lin, T., & L. Yu–Ju. (2015). Language learning in virtual reality environments: Past, present, and future. *Journal of Educational Technology & Society,* 18. (pp. 486–497).

Luchins, A. S. (1942). Mechanization in problem solving. Psychological Monographs, 54, (6, Whole Number 248).

Mandolesi, L., et al. (2018). Effects of physical exercise on cognitive functioning and wellbeing: Biological and psychological benefits. *Frontiers in Psychology*, 9 : 509.

Markman, A., & D. Gentner. (2001). *Thinking, Annual Review of Psychology*, 52. (pp. 223–247).

Marshall, L., & F. Rowland. (2014). *A Guide to Learning Independently*. French Forest, NSW: Pearson Australia.

Mayer, R. E. (2002). Rote versus meaningful learning. *Theory Into Practice*, 41. (pp. 226–232).

Mayer, R. E. (2017). Using multimedia for e-learning. *Journal of Computer Assisted Learning*, 33. (pp. 403–423).

McBurney, D. H. (2002). *How to Think Like a Psychologist: Critical Thinking in Psychology* (2nd ed.). New York: Pearson

McGraw Hill Education. (2015). How social media can help students study. 27 July 2018. <https://www.mheducation.com/blog/thought-leadership/how-social-media-can-help-students-study.html>.

Miller, C.M.I. & M. Parlett. (1974). *Up to the Mark: A Study of The Examination Game*. Guildford: Society for Research into Higher Education.

Mischel, W. (2014). *The Marshmallow Test: Why Self-Control is the Engine of Success*. New York: Little, Brown and Company.

Mischel, W., Y. Shoda, & M. L. Rodriguez. (1989). Delay of gratification in children. *Science*, 244. (pp. 933–938).

Miyatsu, T., et al. (2018). Five popular study strategies: Their pitfalls and optimal implementations. *Perspectives on Psychological Science*, 13. (pp. 390–407).

Moran, A. (1996). *The Psychology of Concentration in Sport Performers: A Cognitive Analysis*. Hove, East Sussex: Psychology Press.

Moran, A., & M. O'Connell. (2006). *Timeless Wisdom: What Irish Proverbs Tell Us About Ourselves*. Dublin: UCD Press.

Moran, A., & J. Toner. (2017). *A Critical Introduction to Sport Psychology* (3rd ed.). London: Routledge.

Mueller, P. A., & D. M. Oppenheimer. (2014). The pen is mightier than the keyboard: Advantages of longhand over laptop note taking. *Psychological Science*, 25. (pp. 1159–1168).

Nabokov, V. (1980). *Lectures on literature*. New York : Harcourt Brace Jovanovich.

Nemani, A., et al. (2018). Convergent validation and transfer of learning studies of a virtual reality-based pattern cutting simulator. *Surgical Endoscopy*, 32. (pp. 1265–1272).

Northey, M., & Timney, B. (2015). *Making Sense: A Student's Guide to Research and Writing* (2nd ed.). Oxford: Oxford University Press.

O'Toole, G. (30 Oct. 2013). I Only Write When Inspiration Strikes. Fortunately It Strikes at Nine Every Morning. *Quote Investigator*. (10 Aug. 2018). <https://quoteinvestigator.com/2013/10/30/inspire-nine/>.

Pascal, Blaise. (1995). *Pensées*. London: Penguin.

Pashler, H., et al. (2008). Learning styles: Concepts and evidence. *Psychological Science in the Public Interest*, 9. (pp. 105–119).

Peterson, D. C, & G. S. Mlynarczyk. (2016). Analysis of traditional versus three-dimensional augmented curriculum on anatomical learning outcome measures. *Anat Sci Educ.*, 9. (pp. 529–536).

Piaget, J. (1962). *Play, Dreams and Imitation in Childhood*. New York: Norton.

Plush, H. (2016). Life's like mountaineering – never look down: The wisdom of Sir Edmund Hillary. *The Telegraph*. 1 May 2018. <https://www.telegraph.co.uk/travel/destinations/asia/nepal/articles/quotes-sir-edmund-hillary-first-man-climb-everest/>.

Pomerantz, J. R. (1983). The rubber pencil illusion. *Perception & Psychophysics*, 33. (pp. 365–368).

Pratte, M. S. (2018). Iconic memories die a sudden death. *Psychological Science*, 29. (pp. 877–887).

Putnam, A., V. Sungkhasettee, & H. L. Roediger III. (2016). Optimizing learning in college: Tips from cognitive psychology. *Perspectives on Psychological Science*, 11. (pp. 652–660).

Qureshi, A., et al. (2014). The method of loci as a mnemonic device to facilitate learning in endocrinology leads to improvement in student performance as measured by assessments. *Advances in Physiology Education*, 38. (pp. 140–144).

Race, P., S. Brown, & B. Smith. (2005). *500 Tips on Assessment* (2nd ed.). London: Routledge Falmer.

Raftery, D. (2018). Ubiquitous mobile use: student perspectives on using the VLE on their phone. *Irish Journal of Technology Enhanced Learning*, 3. (pp. 47–57).

Raftery, D., & A. Risquez. (2018). Engaging students through the VLE: comparing like with like using the #VLEIreland student survey. *Irish Journal of Technology Enhanced Learning*, 3. (pp. 24–34).

Ramsey, L. (16 June 2017). Spinach doesn't have as much of a key nutrient needed in your blood as you think. *Business Insider*. 7 June 2018. <http://uk.businessinsider.com/spinach-iron-levels-nutrition-myths-2017-6?r=US&IR=T>.

Raugh, M. R., & Atkinson, R. C. (1975). A mnemonic method for learning a second-language vocabulary. Journal of Educational Psychology, 67. (pp. 1–16).

Rayner, K., et al. (2012). *The Psychology of Reading* (2nd ed.). Hove, East Sussex: Psychology Press.

Rayner, K., et al. (2016). So much to read, so little time: How do we read? And can speed reading help? *Psychological Science in the Public Interest*, 17. (pp. 4–34).

Raugh, M. R., & R. C. Atkinson. (1975). A mnemonic method for learning a second language vocabulary. *Journal of Educational Psychology*, 67. (pp. 1–16).

Reisberg, D. (2016). *Cognition* (6th ed.). New York: W. W.Norton.

Resnick, B. (2018). The 'marshmallow test' said patience was a key to success. A new replication tells us more. 1 July 2018. <https://www. vox.com/science-and-health/2018/6/6/17413000/marshmallow-test-replication-mischel-psychology>.

Rhodes, E. (2017). Guide to university life. *The Psychologist*. 27 May 2018. <https://thepsychologist.bps.org.uk/volume-30/october-2017/psychologist-guide-university-life>.

Richmond, A. S., et al. (2016). *An Evidence-Based Guide to College and University Teaching: Developing the Model Teacher*. London: Routledge.

Robinson, F. P. (1961). *Effective Study*. New York: Harper & Row.

Roediger III, H. L., & J. D. Kapicke. (2006). Test-enhanced learning: Taking memory tests improves long-term retention. *Psychological Science*, 17. (pp. 249–255).

Runcie, C. (10 May 2016). Five famous novels turned down by publishers. *The Telegraph*. 13 June 2018. <https://www.telegraph.co.uk /books/what-to-read/five-famous-novels-turned-down-by-publishers/>.

Rutgers University (2018). Netiquette – often overlooked policy. 27 July 2018. <https://onlinelearning.rutgers.edu/faq/netiquette>.

Shaughnessy, T. M., & M. L. White. (2012). Making macro memorable: The method of loci mnemonic technique in the Economics classroom. *Journal of Economics and Finance Education*, 11. (pp. 131–141).

Shermer, M. (1997). *Why People Believe Weird Things: Pseudoscience, Superstition and Other Confusions of Our Time*. New York: W. H. Freeman.

Sinnott–Armstrong, W., & R. J. Foegelin (2010). *Understanding Arguments: An Introduction to Informal Logic* (8th ed.). Belmont, CA: Cengage.

Skrabanek, P., & J. McCormick. (1989). *Follies and Fallacies in Medicine*. Glasgow: Tarragon Press.

Smyth, M. M., et al. (1994). *Cognition in Action* (2nd ed.). Hove, East Sussex: Lawrence Erlbaum.

Snyder, B.R. (1971). *The Hidden Curriculum*. Cambridge, MA: MIT Press.

Staph, J. (2011). Usain Bolt's key to explosive starts. 21 May 2018. <http://www.stack.com/a/usain-bolts-key-to-explosive-starts>.

Swann, C., et al. (2017). Psychological states underlying excellent performance in sport: Toward an integrated model of flow and clutch states. *Journal of Applied Sport Psychology*, 29. (pp. 375–401).

Symons, C. S., & B. T. Johnson. (1997). The self-reference effect in memory: A meta-analysis. *Psychological Bulletin*, 121. (pp. 371–394).

Szpunar, K. K. (2017). Directing the wandering mind. *Current Directions in Psychological Science*, 26. (pp. 40–44).

Tsaousides, T. (28 Nov. 2017). How to conquer the fear of public speaking. *Psychology Today*. 8 June 2018. <https://www.psychologytoday.com/us/blog/smashing-the-brainblocks/201711/how-conquer-the-fear-public-speaking>.

University College Dublin (2005). Plagiarism Policy and Procedures. 11 June 2018. <https://www.ucd.ie/t4cms/UCD%20Plagiarism%20Policy%20and%20Procedures.pdf>.

University of Cambridge. (20 Apr. 2016). Social media guidelines, version 1.4. 26 July 2018. <https://www.cam.ac.uk/system/files/social_media_guidelines._version_1.4.pdf>.

University of Waterloo. (2018). Online discussions: Tips for students. 27 July 2018. <https://uwaterloo.ca/centre-for-teaching-excellence/teaching-resources/teaching-tips/developing-assignments/blended-learning/online-discussions-tips-students>.

VandenBos, G. R. (2015). *APA Dictionary of Psychology* (2nd ed.). Washington, DC: American Psychological Association. 29 July 2018. <https://dictionary.apa.org>.

Walsh, D., & R. Paul. (1986). *The Goal of Critical Thinking: From Educational Ideal to Educational Reality*. Washington, D.C.: American Federation of Teachers.

Wegner, D. (1994). Ironic processes of mental control. *Psychological Review*, 101. (pp. 34–52).

Williams, M. & D. Penman. (2011). *Mindfulness: A Practical Guide to Finding Peace in a Frantic World*. London: Piatkus.

Wilson, K., & J. H. Korn. (2007) Topical articles: Attention during lectures – beyond ten minutes. *Teaching of Psychology*, 34. (pp. 85–89).

Winerman, L. (2011). Suppressing the 'white bears'. *APA Monitor on Psychology*, 42. (p. 44).

Wyatt, D., et al. (1993). Comprehension strategies, worth, and credibility monitoring, and evaluations: Cold and hot cognition when experts read professional articles that are important to them. *Learning and Individual Differences*, 5. (pp. 49–72).

Zhang, S. (26 July 2017). Why do people have out-of-body experiences? *The Atlantic*. 2 July 2018. <https://www.theatlantic.com/science/archive/2017/07/the-neuroscience-of-out-of-body-experiences/534696/>.

Zielinski, S. (3 Feb. 2014). The secrets of Sherlock's mind palace. 21 June 2018. <https://www.smithsonianmag.com/arts-culture/secrets-sherlocks-mind-palace-180949567/>.

Index

acronyms 140–1
acrostics 141
active learning 1, 3–5, 10, 54–61
    learner 4–5, 52, 54, 78, 80, 168
    questioning 7–10, 120
    reflection 109
activity diary 34–5
advice 11, 13, 18, 35, 43, 58, 196–8
Ahern, L., J. Feller, & T. Nagle 63
Anderson, Chris 50
answers 4–9, 82–6, 192
    answering oral questions 172–3
    plan 157, 182, 188–91, 193–5
anxiety. *See* examinations
assessment 177
    methods 11, 178–80
    preparation 180–93
assignment 149–50
    choice of topic 152–4
    planning 36, 99, 150–4
    presentation 166–75
    researching 154–5
    responding to feedback 165–6
    submitting 164–5
    writing 156–64
assumptions checking 120
attention 26, 50–1, 57, 91–5, 100, 137
augmented reality 68

background music, effects of 28
Bacon, Francis 85
barriers to learning 52–4
Bartlett, F. 108
begging the question 116
behaviour
    change in 3, 18–20, 26
    improve 22–3, 101, 187
    online 65–6
Besson, Luc 113
Bjork, E. L., & R. A. Bjork 39
Bjork, R. A. et al. 55, 126, 139, 182
Bolt, Usain 92–3, 98–9, 187
book design 87–8
Bradbury, N. A. 50
Browne, M. N., & S. M. Keeley 110
Butler, G., N. Grey & T. Hope 37
Butler, H. A., C. Pentoney, & M.
    Bong 105

chunking 127–8, 143, 144
citation. *See* references
cognitive
    communication rules 170
    overload 50, 91
    processes 51, 74–5, 106
comprehension monitoring 8, 76, 85,
    137, 139

computers. *See* laptops
concentration. *See also* distractions
    43, 91–4
    questioning 9, 80
    techniques 97–102
conclusion
    assignment 109
    claim 111, 121–2
    jump to 120
    of lecture 57–8
    writing 157–8, 160, 168–70
context-dependent processes 132
copyright. *See also* plagiarism 66
cramming 34, 38–9, 127, 185
critical thinking 105–10
    check assumptions 116, 119–20
    critical reading 121
    how to improve 110–20
    questioning 9, 83
    rewriting 161
    sources 111–5, 117–8
curiosity 4, 8, 21, 80, 110

daydream 26, 27, 54, 93
de Mestral, George 4
deadline 25, 41, 152, 164–5
deliberate learning 3–4, 6, 93
depth of processing 56, 137, 144
digital resources 61–70
displacement activities. *See also*
    distractions 15
distractions
    common 5, 94–6
    dealing with 40, 54, 57, 97–102
    environment 26–8, 140
    external 94
    internal 95
Dostoevsky, Fyodor 95
Duckworth, A. 17

Ebbinghaus, Hermann 38
editing 161–4
elaborative rehearsal 48, 56, 86,
    135–8, 145

encoding 28, 76, 129–31, 135, 137,
    143, 145
    memory, description of 126–7
environment. *See also* virtual
    learning environment
    distractions 28–9
    retrieval 131–2, 145
    work 26–9, 140
Ericsson, K. A., R. T. Krampe, & C.
    Tesch-Romer 18
essays. *See* assignments
evaluate online sources 69–70
evidence 115–8, 121, 154–5
evidence, anecdotal 115
examinations. *See also* assessment
    anxiety 186–7
    blank 39
    doing your best 180–93
    extenuating circumstances 198
    failure 193–4
    language 192
    MCQ 194–5
    methods 178–80
    post-mortems 196–7
    rest 185
    rubric 181, 188
    strategy 184–93
exercise, benefits of 29, 42–4, 97,
    117, 196

feedback 165–6, 196–7
final draft 161–4
first draft 156–61
flow experiences 93
focus. *See also* concentration 54–5
Foer, Joshua 142
FOMO 20, 95
footnotes 152, 163
foresight bias 182
Forster, E. M. 186

Gauss, Carl Frederick 107
Gazzaniga, M. 22, 106, 109, 110,
    133, 134

generative processing 53
Gilovich, T. 114
Gladwell, M. 18
goal
    goal-setting 37–8, 42–3
    study goals 18, 22–6, 41
Godden, D. R., & A. D. Baddeley
    132
Goodwin, D. W., et al. 132
Google search how to evaluate. *See*
    websites
grit 16–7
Gruber, M. J., at al. 80
Gruneberg, M. M., & G. D. Jacobs
    143

Hamblin, T. J. 116
hashtag 63
heading 8, 56, 65, 80, 88, 136–8,
    145–6, 174
Hillary, Sir Edmund 21
Holmes, Oliver Wendell 126
Holmes, Sherlock 142
Husmann, P. R., & V. D. O'Loughlin
    113

inferences, drawing 75, 77
information. *See* evidence
interactivity 48, 61–2, 67
introduction, writing an 159–60, 168
ironic processes 95–6

James, William 15, 39, 135

keyword method mnemonic 143
keywords 65, 143
knowledge-based effect 126–8, 145
Kosslyn, S. M., communication
    rules for slides 166–70

Lannin, D. G., & N. A. Scott 62
laptop 5, 53, 61, 94, 169
law of effect 22
Leadsom, Andrea 117

learning *See also* state dependency
    barriers to 52–4
    by rote 140–6
    deliberate and incidental 3–4, 6,
        93
    skills 12
    style 112–3
lecture
    barriers to learning from 52–4
    challenge of 49–51
    getting the most out of 5, 54–60
    notes 55, 58
    recording 60
    routine 38
listening 13, 28, 48, 50–4, 58, 92,
    171

marking. *See* underlining
marshmallow challenge 20
May, Theresa 117
Mayer, R. E. 61, 125
MCQ. *See* multiple choice questions
means-end analysis 99
memory
    chunking 127–8
    encoding 28, 76, 129–31, 135,
        137, 145
    for faces 129
    for numbers 127–8
    iconic 134
    improvement techniques 136–44
    long-term 116, 133, 135–6, 139,
        145
    principles of remembering 144–5
    retrieval 28, 131–3, 137–9, 145,
        183
    sensory 133–4
    short-term. *See* working memory
    stages of 129–33
    storage 131
    stores 133–6
    trace 129, 142
    working 47, 51, 77, 91–2, 108,
        134–5, 138, 144

mental skills
   control 95–6
   health 5
   processes 51, 76
   reading 75–8
   rehearsal 101–2
   spotlight 9, 92–4
   thinking 106–8
method of loci mnemonic 142
mind palace mnemonic 143–4
mindfulness
   meditation 96
   mindful awareness 100–2
   mindful practice 18
mnemonics 140–44
Moran, Aidan 21, 24, 29, 54, 94, 97, 101
motivation
   achievement 19
   affiliation 19
   how to increase 22–30
   intrinsic, extrinsic (push, pull) 18–20
   to attend university 16–7
   types of 19–21
motives 18–20
multiple choice questions 18–20, 194–5

Nabokov, Vladimir 73, 156
netiquette 65
neuromyths 112–3
noisy environment 27–8
Norgay, Tensing 21
notes. *See also* lecture notes 47–8, 52–60

O'Connell, M. 29
organisation 53, 64, 85–6, 138, 144, 157–8, 162
out-of-body experiences 119
overlearning 40, 130, 144

papers. *See* assignments
Parker, Dorothy 166

Pasteur, Louis 116
performance 54–5, 93
Peterson, D. C, & G. S. Mlynarczyk 68
phone 5, 25, 27, 60, 94–5
photocopying 85
Piaget, Jean 127
place to study. *See* work environment
plagiarism 62, 67, 140, 155, 156
plan 150–4, 156–7, 167, 181, 190
positive reinforcement 22
PQRR reading technique 79–84, 137
   previewing 79–80
   questioning 80–2, 131
   reading 82–3
   reviewing 83
   revision 181
practice
   deliberate 17–8
   distributed 38–9, 59, 127, 183
   generic and mindful 18
   massed. *See* cramming
preparation. *See* revision
presentation
   oral 149–50, 166–73
   poster 173–5
   style 162–3
previewing 79–80, 84
primacy effect 167
privacy settings 65
processing, deepest level 130–1, 135, 144
procrastination 35–6
punishment 23
Putnam, A. 5, 26, 33, 39, 52, 59, 183

questions
   active 4–5, 80–2, 86
   answering an audience 172–3
   critical thinking 109–20
   exam questions 181–4, 188–95
   importance of 7–10, 93–4, 144
   listening 51, 54, 56

overlearn 130
research 150–4
study 23–4, 29, 35, 59, 137

Raugh, M. R., & Atkinson, R. C. 143
reading critically 121
reading lists 78–9
reading. *See* PQRR technique
recency effect 167
recording 60
references 58–9, 69, 78, 88, 155, 161, 163–4
rehearsal
    elaborative 48, 56, 86, 135–8, 145
    maintenance 131, 135, 144
remembering. *See also* memory
    mnemonics 140–44
    principles of 144–5
repetition 38–9, 52, 131, 135, 140–4
research. *See also* questions
    assignments 154–5
    evidence 115–8, 121, 154–5
    planning and writing 152–5
    topic 152–4
rest, exams 185
retrieval 28, 131–3, 137–9, 145, 183
    testing effect 139
reviewing 59–60, 83–4, 144, 181
revision plan 181
reward 20–3, 36
Robinson, Francis 79
rote learning 125, 140–1, 143, 144
routines 15, 22, 26–30, 38
    examinations 186–7
    pre-lecture 54–5
    pre-performance 97
    study 97–8
Rowling, J. K. 166
rubbery pencil effect 134

Sadow, Bernard 4
Sartre, Jean-Paul 136
scepticism, amiable 110–20
schemas. *See also* headings 135–6, 145

scope and limitations 157, 159, 160, 161
seduction of reproduction 85
self-control 20–1
self-reference effect 9–10
Shaw, George Bernard 39
Shermer, M. 111
signpost words 54, 58, 80, 157, 164, 190
Simonides of Ceos 142
Skinner, B. F. 22
slides (PowerPoint) 167–71
SMART. *See also* goal-setting 23–4, 37, 154
Smyth, M. M., et al. 51
social media 5, 15, 26, 62–5, 94–5, 111
source. *See also* evidence
    critical thinking 111–5, 117–8
    evaluate online 69–70
    primary and secondary 79, 114
spaced practice. *See* distributed practice
state dependency learning 132–3, 145
state-specific recall 132
stress 41
study
    duration 39–40
    goals 18, 22–6, 41
    group 63–7, 139–40
    priorities 34–5
    routine 97–8
subliminal advertising 112
submitting 164–5
successful students 8, 54, 61, 77–8
summary 85–6, 160
    summary sheet 37, 40, 43, 83, 84, 137, 182–6
syllabus 181, 183

target audience 69
task-hopping 36
Taylor, Phil 21
TED talks 50

textbooks. *See also* reading; book
    design
    how to read 77–8
    learning from 85–6
thinking. *See also* critical thinking
    abstract 125, 146
    creative 107–8
    for yourself 73, 105, 109–10, 119,
        199
    thought suppression 96
Thorndike, Edward Lee 22
time
    run out of 193
    study 29, 33–7, 40–1, 43
    time management. *See also*
        distributed study; deadline
        assessing use of time 34
        examinations 188–91, 194–5
        priorities 41–2
        techniques 29
        timetable 40, 42–3
    time-wasting. *See* procrastination
    traffic light 29, 42
    travel 37, 40, 183
tip of the tongue phenomenon 132
Toner, J. 21, 101
topic 40, 60, 152–4, 181–3
transcription, verbatim 48, 52–3, 55, 85
transition
    to university 4–5
    words/phrases 158, 164, 190

trigger words 100

underlining 85
understanding 3–4, 125–7, 131,
    135–40
    principles of 144–5
university, going to 1–6, 12
urban myths 111–12

Vettel, Sebastian 101
virtual learning environment 48–9,
    52, 61–8
virtual reality 68

wasting time. *See* procrastination
Wegner, D. 96
wesite evaluating 69–70
Wilson, K., & J. H. Korn 50
work environment 26–9, 140
writing
    conclusions 157–8, 160,
        168–70
    editing 161–4
    final draft 161–4
    first draft 156–61
    introduction 159–60, 168
    main body of text 160
    organising material 158–9
    preliminary outline 157–8
    summary 160
Wyatt, D., et al. 77